Informing the legislative debate since 1914 _____

Navy Force Structure and Shipbuilding Plans: Background and Issues for Congress

Ronald O'Rourke
Specialist in Naval Affairs

November 8, 2013

Congressional Research Service

7-5700

www.crs.gov

RL32665

Summary

The Navy's proposed FY2014 budget requests funding for the procurement of 8 new battle force ships (i.e., ships that count against the Navy's goal for achieving and maintaining a fleet of 306 ships). The 8 ships include two Virginia-class attack submarines, one DDG-51 class Aegis destroyer, four Littoral Combat Ships (LCSs), and one Mobile Landing Platform/Afloat Forward Staging Base (MLP/AFSB) ship. The Navy's proposed FY2014-FY2018 five-year shipbuilding plan includes a total of 41 ships—the same number as in the Navy's FY213-FY2017 five-year shipbuilding plan, and one less than the 42 ships that the Navy planned for FY2014-FY2018 under the FY2013 budget submission.

The planned size of the Navy, the rate of Navy ship procurement, and the prospective affordability of the Navy's shipbuilding plans have been matters of concern for the congressional defense committees for the past several years. The Navy's FY2014 30-year (FY2014-FY2043) shipbuilding plan, like the Navy's previous 30-year shipbuilding plans in recent years, does not include enough ships to fully support all elements of the Navy's 306-ship goal over the long run. The Navy projects that the fleet would remain below 306 ships during most of the 30-year period, and experience shortfalls at various points in cruisers-destroyers, attack submarines, and amphibious ships.

In its October 2013 report on the cost of the FY2014 30-year shipbuilding plan, the Congressional Budget Office (CBO) estimates that the plan would cost an average of $19.3 billion per year in constant FY2013 dollars to implement, or about 15% more than the Navy estimates. CBO's estimate is about 6% higher than the Navy's estimate for the first 10 years of the plan, about 14% higher than the Navy's estimate for the second 10 years of the plan, and about 26% higher than the Navy's estimate for the final 10 years of the plan. Some of the difference between CBO's estimate and the Navy's estimate, particularly in the latter years of the plan, is due to a difference between CBO and the Navy in how to treat inflation in Navy shipbuilding.

Proposed issues for Congress in reviewing the Navy's proposed FY2014 shipbuilding budget, its proposed FY2014-FY2018 five-year shipbuilding plan, and its FY2014 30-year (FY2014-FY2043) shipbuilding plan include the following:

- the impact on Navy shipbuilding programs of the March 1, 2013, sequester on FY2013 funding and unobligated prior-year funding;
- the potential impact on Navy shipbuilding programs of a possible sequester later this year or early next year on FY2014 funding and unobligated prior-year funding;
- the potential impact on the size of the Navy of reducing DOD spending (through sequestration or regular appropriations activity) in FY2013-FY2021 to levels at or near the lower caps established in the Budget Control Act of 2011;
- the future size and structure of the Navy in light of strategic and budgetary changes;
- the sufficiency of the 30-year shipbuilding plan for achieving the Navy's goal for a 306-ship fleet; and
- the affordability of the 30-year shipbuilding plan.

Funding levels and legislative activity on individual Navy shipbuilding programs are tracked in detail in other CRS reports.

Contents

Tables

Appendixes

Contacts

Introduction

This report provides background information and presents potential issues for Congress concerning the Navy's ship force-structure goals and shipbuilding plans. The planned size of the Navy, the rate of Navy ship procurement, and the prospective affordability of the Navy's shipbuilding plans have been matters of concern for the congressional defense committees for the past several years. Decisions that Congress makes on Navy shipbuilding programs can substantially affect Navy capabilities and funding requirements, and the U.S. shipbuilding industrial base.

Background

Navy's Ship Force Structure Goal

January 2013 Goal for Fleet of 306 Ships

On January 31, 2013, in response to Section 1015 of the FY2013 National Defense Authorization Act (H.R. 4310/P.L. 112-239 of January 2, 2013), the Navy submitted to Congress a report presenting a goal for achieving and maintaining a fleet of 306 ships, consisting of certain types and quantities of ships.[1] The goal for a 306-ship fleet is the result of a force structure assessment (FSA) that the Navy completed in 2012.

306-Ship Goal Reflects 2012 Strategic Guidance and Projected DOD Spending Shown in FY2013 and FY2014 Budget Submissions

The 2012 FSA and the resulting 306-ship plan reflect the defense strategic guidance document that the Administration presented in January 2012[2] and the associated projected levels of Department of Defense (DOD) spending shown in the FY2013 and FY2014 budget submissions. DOD officials have stated that if planned levels of DOD spending are reduced below what is shown in these budget submissions, the defense strategy set forth in the January 2012 strategic guidance document might need to be changed. Such a change, Navy officials have indicated, could lead to the replacement of the 306-ship plan of January 2013 with a new plan.

Goal for Fleet of 306 Ships Compared to Earlier Goals

Table 1 compares the 306-ship goal to earlier Navy ship force structure plans.

---

[1] Department of the Navy, *Report to Congress [on] Navy Combatant Vessel Force Structure Requirement*, January 2013, 3 pp. The cover letters for the report were dated January 31, 2013.

[2] For more on this document, see CRS Report R42146, *In Brief: Assessing the January 2012 Defense Strategic Guidance (DSG)*, by Catherine Dale and Pat Towell.

Table 1. Current 306 Ship Force Structure Goal Compared to Earlier Goals

Ship type	306-ship plan of January 2013	~310-316 ship plan of March 2012	Revised 313-ship plan of September 2011	Changes to February 2006 313-ship plan announced through mid-2011	February 2006 Navy plan for 313-ship fleet	Early-2005 Navy plan for fleet of 260-325 ships		2002-2004 Navy plan for 375-ship Navy[a]	2001 QDR plan for 310-ship Navy
						260-ships	325-ships		
Ballistic missile submarines (SSBNs)	12[b]	12-14[b]	12[b]	12[b]	14	14	14	14	14
Cruise missile submarines (SSGNs)	0[c]	0-4[c]	4[c]	0[c]	4	4	4	4	2 or 4[d]
Attack submarines (SSNs)	48	~48	48	48	48	37	41	55	55
Aircraft carriers	11[e]	11[e]	11[e]	11[e]	11[f]	10	11	12	12
Cruisers and destroyers	88	~90	94	94[g]	88	67	92	104	116
Frigates	0	0	0	0	0	0	0	0	
Littoral Combat Ships (LCSs)	52	~55	55	55	55	63	82	56	0
Amphibious ships	33	~32	33	33[h]	31	17	24	37	36
MPF(F) ships[i]	0[i]	0[i]	0[i]	0[i]	12[i]	14[i]	20[i]	0[i]	0[i]
Combat logistics (resupply) ships	29	~29	30	30	30	24	26	42	34
Dedicated mine warfare ships	0	0	0	0	0	0	0	26[k]	16
Joint High Speed Vessels (JHSVs)	10[l]	10[l]	10[l]	21[l]	3	0	0	0	0
Other[m]	23	~23	16	24[n]	17	10	11	25	25
Total battle force ships	306	~310-316	313	328	313	260	325	375	310 or 312

Sources: Table prepared by CRS based on U.S. Navy data.

Note: QDR is Quadrennial Defense Review. The "~" symbol means approximately and signals that the number in question may be refined as a result of the Naval Force Structure Assessment currently in progress.

a. Initial composition. Composition was subsequently modified.

b. The Navy plans to replace the 14 current Ohio-class SSBNs with a new class of 12 next-generation SSBNs. For further discussion, see CRS Report R41129, *Navy Ohio Replacement (SSBN[X]) Ballistic Missile Submarine Program: Background and Issues for Congress*, by Ronald O'Rourke.

c. Although the Navy plans to continue operating its four SSGNs until they reach retirement age in the late 2020s, the Navy does not plan to replace these ships when they retire. This situation can be expressed in a table like this one with either a 4 or a zero.

d. The report on the 2001 QDR did not mention a specific figure for SSGNs. The Administration's proposed FY2001 DOD budget requested funding to support the conversion of two available Trident SSBNs into SSGNs, and the retirement of two other Trident SSBNs. Congress, in marking up this request, supported a plan to convert all four available SSBNs into SSGNs.

e. With congressional approval, the goal has been temporarily be reduced to 10 carriers for the period between the retirement of the carrier *Enterprise* (CVN-65) in December 2012 and entry into service of the carrier *Gerald R. Ford* (CVN-78), currently scheduled for September 2015.

f. For a time, the Navy characterized the goal as 11 carriers in the nearer term, and eventually 12 carriers.

g. The 94-ship goal was announced by the Navy in an April 2011 report to Congress on naval force structure and missile defense.

h. The Navy acknowledged that meeting a requirement for being able to lift the assault echelons of 2.0 Marine Expeditionary Brigades (MEBs) would require a minimum of 33 amphibious ships rather than the 31 ships shown in the February 2006 plan. For further discussion, see CRS Report RL34476, *Navy LPD-17 Amphibious Ship Procurement: Background, Issues, and Options for Congress*, by Ronald O'Rourke.

i. Today's Maritime Prepositioning Force (MPF) ships are intended primarily to support Marine Corps operations ashore, rather than Navy combat operations, and thus are not counted as Navy battle force ships. The planned MPF (Future) ships, however, would have contributed to Navy combat capabilities (for example, by supporting Navy aircraft operations). For this reason, the ships in the planned MPF(F) squadron were counted by the Navy as battle force ships. The planned MPF(F) squadron was subsequently restructured into a different set of initiatives for enhancing the existing MPF squadrons; the Navy no longer plans to acquire an MPF(F) squadron.

j. The Navy no longer plans to acquire an MPF(F) squadron. The Navy, however, has procured or plans to procure some of the ships that were previously planned for the squadron—specifically, TAKE-1 class cargo ships, and Mobile Landing Platform (MLP)/Afloat Forward Staging Base (AFSB) ships. These ships are included in the total shown for "Other" ships.

k. The figure of 26 dedicated mine warfare ships included 10 ships maintained in a reduced mobilization status called Mobilization Category B. Ships in this status are not readily deployable and thus do not count as battle force ships. The 375-ship proposal thus implied transferring these 10 ships to a higher readiness status.

l. Totals shown include 5 ships transferred from the Army to the Navy and operated by the Navy primarily for the performance of Army missions.

m. This category includes, among other things, command ships and support ships.

n. The increase in this category from 17 ships under the February 2006 313-ship plan to 24 ships under the apparent 328-ship goal included the addition of one TAGOS ocean surveillance ship and the transfer into this category of six ships—three modified TAKE-1 class cargo ships, and three Mobile Landing Platform (MLP) ships—that were previously intended for the planned (but now canceled) MPF(F) squadron.

Navy's Five-Year and 30-Year Shipbuilding Plans

Five-Year (FY2014-FY2018) Shipbuilding Plan

Table 2 shows the Navy's FY2014 five-year (FY2013-FY2018) shipbuilding plan.

Table 2. Navy FY2014 Five-Year (FY2014-FY2018) Shipbuilding Plan

(Battle force ships—i.e., ships that count against 306-ship goal)

Ship type	FY14	FY15	FY16	FY17	FY18	Total
Ford (CVN-78) class aircraft carrier	0	0	0	0	1	1
Virginia (SSN-774) class attack submarine	2	2	2	2	2	10
Arleigh Burke (DDG-51) class destroyer	1	2	2	2	2	9
Littoral Combat Ship (LCS)	4	4	2	2	2	14
LHA(R) amphibious assault ship	0	0	0	1	0	1
Fleet tug (TATF)	0	0	0	2	1	3
Mobile Landing Platform (MLP)/Afloat Forward Staging Base (AFSB)	1	0	0	0	0	1
TAO(X) oiler	0	0	1	0	1	2
TOTAL	**8**	**8**	**7**	**9**	**9**	**41**

Source: FY2014 Navy budget submission.

Notes: The MLP/AFSB is a variant of the MLP with additional features permitting it to serve in the role of an AFSB. The Navy proposes to fund the TATFs and TAO(X)s through the National Defense Sealift Fund (NDSF) and the other ships through the Navy's shipbuilding account, known formally as the Shipbuilding and Conversion, Navy (SCN) appropriation account.

Observations that can be made about the Navy's proposed five-year (FY2014-FY2018) shipbuilding plan include the following:

- **Total of 41 ships—about the same as last year.** The Navy's proposed FY2014-FY2018 five-year shipbuilding plan includes a total of 41 ships—the same number as in the Navy's FY213-FY2017 five-year shipbuilding plan, and one less than the 42 ships that the Navy planned for FY2014-FY2018 under the FY2013 budget submission.

- **Average of 8.2 ships per year.** The FY2013-FY2017 plan includes an average of 8.2 battle force ships per year. The steady-state replacement rate for a fleet of 306 ships with an average service life of 35 years is about 8.7 ships per year. In light of how the average shipbuilding rate since FY1993 has been substantially below 8.7 ships per year (see **Appendix D**), shipbuilding supporters for some time have wanted to increase the shipbuilding rate to a steady rate of 10 or more battle force ships per year.

- **Second Virginia-class submarine added in FY2014.** Compared to the FY2013-FY2017 five-year shipbuilding plan, the FY2014-FY2018 five-year shipbuilding plan adds a second Virginia-class attack submarine in FY2014. This follows through on Congress's action, in marking up the FY2013 budget, to provide advance procurement funding in FY2013 for a second Virginia-class boat in FY2014.

- **One DDG-51 destroyer in FY2014.** The FY2014-FY2018 five-year shipbuilding plan, like the FY2013-FY2017 five-year shipbuilding plan, includes one DDG-51 destroyer in FY2014. During Congress's review of the Navy's FY2013 budget submission, there was interest in Congress in adding a second DDG-51 destroyer to FY2014. In final action, Congress instead procured an additional DDG-51 destroyer in FY2013 (increasing the number of DDG-51s procured in FY2013 to three, compared to the two that were requested for FY2013). The third DDG-51 procured in FY2013 might be viewed as the equivalent of the second DDG-51 that supporters wanted to add to FY2014.

- **Start of LX(R) amphibious ship procurement deferred beyond FY2018.** The proposed FY2014-FY2018 five-year shipbuilding plan defers the procurement of the first LX(R) amphibious ship from FY2018 to a later fiscal year. The FY2013-FY2017 five-year shipbuilding plan had deferred the ship from FY2017 to FY2018. LX(R)s (previously designated LSD[X]s) are to replace aging LSD-41/49 class amphibious ships.

30-Year (FY2014-FY2043) Shipbuilding Plan

Table 3 shows the Navy's FY2014 30-year (FY2014-FY2043) shipbuilding plan, the tables for which were submitted to Congress on April 22, 2012.

Table 3. Navy FY2014 30-Year (FY2014-FY2043) Shipbuilding Plan

FY	CVN	LSC	SSC	SSN	SSBN	AWS	CLF	Supt	Total
14		1	4	2				1	8
15		2	4	2					8
16		2	2	2			1		7
17		2	2	2		1		2	9
18	1	2	2	2			1	1	9
19		2	3	2		1	1	1	10
20		2	3	2			1	2	10
21		2	3	2	1	1	1		10
22		3	3	2			1	2	11
23	1	3	3	2		1	1	3	14
24		2	3	1	1	1	1	2	11
25		3	3	2		1	1	1	11
26		2	1	1	1		1		6
27		3		2	1	1	1		8
28	1	3		1	1	2	1	1	10
29		3		1	1	1	1	1	8
30		2	1	1	1	1	1	2	9
31		2		2	1	1	1	2	9
32		2	1	1	1	2	1	3	11
33	1	2		1	1	1	1	2	9
34		2	1	1	1			2	7
35		2	1	1	1				5
36		2		1		1			4
37		2	4	2					8
38	1	3	4	2					10
39		3	4	1					8
40		3	4	2		2			11
41		3	4	1					8
42		3	3	2		1			9
43	1	2	3	1			1		8

Source: FY2014 30-year (FY2014-FY2043) shipbuilding plan.

Key: FY = Fiscal Year; **CVN** = aircraft carriers; **LSC** = surface combatants (i.e., cruisers and destroyers); **SSC** = small surface combatants (i.e., Littoral Combat Ships [LCSs]); **SSN** = attack submarines; **SSGN** = cruise missile submarines; **SSBN** = ballistic missile submarines; **AWS** = amphibious warfare ships; **CLF** = combat logistics force (i.e., resupply) ships; **Supt** = support ships.

In devising a 30-year shipbuilding plan to move the Navy toward its ship force-structure goal, key assumptions and planning factors include but are not limited to the following:

- ship service lives;
- estimated ship procurement costs;
- projected shipbuilding funding levels; and
- industrial-base considerations.

The Navy states that

> This [FY2014] 30-year shipbuilding plan is based on these key assumptions:

— [A] Battle Force inventory of the "2012 Navy FSA [Force Structure Assessment]" [i.e., of 306 ships] will remain the objective of this plan.

— In the near term [i.e., FY2014-FY2023], the Annual budget for Navy shipbuilding will be sustained at the levels of the FY14 President's Budget (PB14) [i.e., the Navy's proposed FY2014 budget] through the Future Year Defense Plan (FYDP) [i.e., during FY2014-Fy2018]. In the med-term [i.e., FY2024-FY2033], [the] annual budget will remain at appropriate (higher) levels; and in the far term [i.e., FY2034-FY2043], [it will] be sustained at appropriate levels (slightly higher than [the] current historical average).

— All battle force ships serve to the end of the planned or extended lives.

— The DoN [Department of the Navy] will continue to acquire and build ships in the most affordable manner.[3]

Navy's Projected Force Levels Under 30-Year Shipbuilding Plan

Table 4 shows the Navy's projection of force levels for FY2014-FY2043 that would result from implementing the FY2014 30-year (FY2014-FY2043) shipbuilding plan shown in **Table 3**.

---

[3] *Report to Congress on the Annual Long-Range Plan for Construction of Naval Vessels for FY2014*, May 2013, p. 4.

Table 4. Projected Force Levels Resulting from FY2014 30-Year (FY2014-FY2043) Shipbuilding Plan

	CVN	LSC	SSC	SSN	SSGN	SSBN	AWS	CLF	Supt	Total
306 ship plan	11	88	52	48	0	12	33	29	33	306
FY14	10	85	26	55	4	14	31	31	26	282
FY15	10	78	23	55	4	14	28	29	29	270
FY16	11	82	27	53	4	14	29	29	31	280
FY17	11	83	29	50	4	14	30	29	33	283
FY18	11	84	33	52	4	14	31	29	33	291
FY19	11	86	38	52	4	14	31	29	35	300
FY20	11	87	37	49	4	14	31	29	33	295
FY21	11	88	37	49	4	14	31	29	33	296
FY22	12	87	39	48	4	14	31	29	33	297
FY23	12	87	38	48	4	14	31	29	34	297
FY24	12	89	40	48	4	14	32	29	34	302
FY25	11	88	42	47	4	14	34	29	34	303
FY26	11	89	45	46	2	14	33	29	33	302
FY27	11	91	48	45	1	13	33	29	33	304
FY28	11	90	51	43	0	12	33	29	33	302
FY29	11	88	52	42	0	11	33	29	33	299
FY30	11	86	52	43	0	11	32	29	33	297
FY31	11	82	52	44	0	11	32	29	33	294
FY32	11	81	52	45	0	10	32	29	34	294
FY33	11	81	52	46	0	10	33	29	34	296
FY34	11	80	52	47	0	10	34	29	34	297
FY35	11	82	52	48	0	10	33	29	34	299
FY36	11	84	52	50	0	10	33	29	34	303
FY37	11	86	52	51	0	10	34	29	33	306
FY38	11	88	52	50	0	10	33	29	34	307
FY39	11	90	52	50	0	10	33	29	33	308
FY40	10	90	52	50	0	10	32	29	33	308
FY41	10	90	52	49	0	11	33	29	33	307
FY42	10	88	52	51	0	12	32	29	33	307
FY43	10	88	52	51	0	12	31	29	33	306

Source: FY2014 30-year (FY2014-FY2043) shipbuilding plan.

Note: Figures for support ships include five JHSVs transferred from the Army to the Navy and operated by the Navy primarily for the performance of Army missions.

Key: FY = Fiscal Year; CVN = aircraft carriers; LSC = surface combatants (i.e., cruisers and destroyers); SSC = small surface combatants (i.e., frigates, Littoral Combat Ships [LCSs], and mine warfare ships); SSN = attack submarines; SSGN = cruise missile submarines; SSBN = ballistic missile submarines; AWS = amphibious warfare ships; CLF = combat logistics force (i.e., resupply) ships; Supt = support ships.

Observations that can be made about the Navy's FY2014 30-year (FY2014-FY2043) shipbuilding plan and resulting projected force levels included the following:

- **Total of 266 ships; average of about 8.9 per year.** The plan includes a total of 266 ships to be procured, two less than the number in the FY2013 30-year (FY2013-FY2042) shipbuilding plan. The total of 266 ships equates to an average of about 8.9 ships per year, which is slightly higher than the approximate average procurement rate (sometimes called the steady-state replacement rate) of about 8.7 ships per year that would be needed over the long run to achieve and maintain a fleet of 306 ships, assuming an average life of 35 years for Navy ships.

- **Projected fleet remains below 306 ships.** Although the FY2014 30-year plan includes an average of about 8.9 ships per year, the FY2014 30-year plan, like previous 30-year plans, results in a fleet that does not fully support all elements of the Navy's ship force structure goal over the 30-year period. The distribution of the 266 ships over the 30-year period, combined with the ages of the Navy's existing ships, results in a projected fleet that would remain below 306 ships during most of the 30-year period and experience shortfalls at various points in cruisers-destroyers, attack submarines, and amphibious ships.

- **Ballistic missile submarine force to be reduced temporarily to 10 boats.** As a result of a decision in the FY2013 budget to defer the scheduled procurement of the first Ohio replacement (SSBN[X]) ballistic missile submarine by two years, from FY2019 to FY2021, the ballistic missile submarine force is projected to drop to a total of 10 or 11 boats—one or two boats below the 12-boat SSBN force-level goal—during the period FY2029-FY2041. The Navy says this reduction is acceptable for meeting current strategic nuclear deterrence mission requirements, because none of the 10 or 11 boats during these years will be encumbered by long-term maintenance.[4]

- **Seven CG-47 class cruisers and two LSD-41 class ships again proposed for early retirement.** The Navy's FY2013 budget submission proposed the early retirements in FY2013 and FY2014 of seven CG-47 class Aegis cruisers and two LSD-41 class amphibious ships. Congress, in acting on the Navy's proposed FY2013 budget, did not accept this proposal, and instead instructed the Navy to keep these nine ships in service. Section 8103 of the FY2013 DOD appropriations act (Division C of H.R. 933/P.L. 113-6 of March 26, 2013, the Consolidated and Further Continuing Appropriations Act, 2013) established a Ship Modernization, Operations and Sustainment Fund to fund the continued operation and support of these nine ships in FY2013 and FY2014. The Navy's FY2014 30-year shipbuilding plan again proposes the early retirements of seven CG-47 class Aegis cruisers and two LSD-41 class amphibious ships, with the retirement to occur in FY2015. The exact cruisers and amphibious ships to be retired under the Navy's FY2014 submission might differ from the exact cruisers and amphibious ships to be retired under the Navy's FY2013 budget submission, but the general idea of having early retirements for seven CG-47 class cruisers and two LSD-41 class amphibious appears to be the same, except that the early

---

[4] For further discussion of this issue, see CRS Report R41129, *Navy Ohio Replacement (SSBN[X]) Ballistic Missile Submarine Program: Background and Issues for Congress*, by Ronald O'Rourke.

retirements would now occur in FY2015 (i.e., one year beyond the two-year window funded by Section 8103).

Comparison of First 10 Years of 30-Year Plans

Table 5 and **Table 6** below show the first 10 years of planned annual ship procurement quantities and projected Navy force sizes in 30-year shipbuilding plans dating back to the first such plan, which was submitted in 2000 in conjunction with the FY2001 budget. By reading vertically down each column, one can see how the ship procurement quantity or Navy force size projected for a given fiscal year changed as that year drew closer to becoming the current budget year.

Table 5. Ship Procurement Quantities in First 10 Years of 30-Year Shipbuilding Plans

Years shown are fiscal years

FY of 30-year plan (year submitted)	01	02	03	04	05	06	07	08	09	10	11	12	13	14	15	16	17	18	19	20	21	22	23
FY01 plan (2000)	8	8	8	8	7	5	6	6	6	7													
FY02 plan (2001)		6	n/a	n/a	n/a	n/a	n/a	n/a	n/a	n/a	n/a	n/a											
FY03 plan (2002)			5	5	7	7	11	n/a	n/a	n/a	n/a	n/a											
FY04 plan (2003)				7	8	7	7	9	14	15	13	14	15										
FY05 plan (2004)					9	6	8	9	17	14	15	14	16	15									
FY06 plan (2005)						4	7	7	9	10	12	n/a	n/a	n/a	n/a								
FY07 plan (2006)							7	7	11	12	14	13	12	11	11	10							
FY08 plan (2007)								7	11	12	13	12	12	10	12	11	6						
FY09 plan (2008)									7	8	8	12	12	13	13	12	12	13					
FY10 plan (2009)										8	n/a	n/a	n/a	n/a	n/a	n/a	n/a	n/a	n/a				
FY11 plan (2010)											9	8	12	9	12	9	12	9	13	9			
FY12 plan (2011)												10	13	11	12	9	12	10	12	8	9		
FY13 plan (2012)													10	7	8	9	7	11	8	12	9	12	
FY14 plan (2013)														8	8	7	9	9	10	10	10	11	14

Source: Navy 30-year shipbuilding plans supplemented by annual Navy budget submissions (including 5-year shipbuilding plans) for fiscal years shown. **n/a** means not available—see notes below.

Notes: The FY2001 30-year plan submitted in 2000 was submitted under a one-time-only legislative provision, Section 1013 of the FY2000 National Defense Authorization Act (S. 1059/P.L. 106-65 of October 5, 1999). No provision required DOD to submit a 30-year shipbuilding plan in 2001 or 2002, when Congress considered DOD's proposed FY2002 and FY2003 DOD budgets. (In addition, no FYDP was submitted in 2001, the first year of the George W. Bush Administration.) Section 1022 of the FY2003 Bob Stump National Defense Authorization Act (H.R. 4546/P.L. 107-314 of December 2, 2002) created a requirement to submit a 30-year shipbuilding plan each year, in conjunction with each year's defense budget. This provision was codified at 10 U.S.C. 231. The first 30-year plan submitted under this provision was the one submitted in 2003, in conjunction with the proposed FY2004 DOD budget. For the next several years, 30-year shipbuilding plans were submitted each year, in conjunction with each year's proposed DOD budget. An exception occurred in 2009, the first year of the Obama Administration, when DOD submitted a proposed budget for FY2010 with no accompanying FYDP or 30-year Navy shipbuilding plan. Section 1023 of the FY2011 Ike Skelton National Defense Authorization Act (H.R. 6523/P.L. 111-383 of January 7, 2011) amended 10 U.S.C. 231 to require DOD to submit a 30-year shipbuilding plan once every four years, in the same year that

DOD submits a Quadrennial Defense Review (QDR). Consistent with Section 1023, DOD did not submit a new 30-year shipbuilding plan at the time that it submitted the proposed FY2012 DOD budget. At the request of the House Armed Services Committee, the Navy submitted the FY2012 30-year (FY2012-FY2041) shipbuilding plan in late-May 2011. Section 1011 of the FY2012 National Defense Authorization Act (H.R. 1540/P.L. 112-81 of December 31, 2011) amended 10 U.S.C. 231 to reinstate the requirement to submit a 30-year shipbuilding plan each year, in conjunction with each year's defense budget.

Table 6. Projected Navy Force Sizes in First 10 years of 30-Year Shipbuilding Plans

Years shown are fiscal years

FY of 30-year plan (year submitted)	01	02	03	04	05	06	07	08	09	10	11	12	13	14	15	16	17	18	19	20	21	22	23
FY01 plan (2000)	316	315	313	313	313	311	311	304	305	305													
FY02 plan (2001)		316	n/a	n/a	n/a	n/a	n/a	n/a	n/a	n/a	n/a												
FY03 plan (2002)			314	n/a	n/a	n/a	n/a	n/a	n/a	n/a	n/a	n/a											
FY04 plan (2003)				292	292	291	296	301	305	308	313	317	321										
FY05 plan (2004)					290	290	298	303	308	307	314	320	328	326									
FY06 plan (2005)						289	293	297	301	306	n/a	n/a	n/a	305	n/a								
FY07 plan (2006)							285	294	299	301	306	315	317	315	314	n/a							
FY08 plan (2007)								286	286	289	293	302	310	311	307	314	317	322					
FY09 plan (2008)									286	287	289	290	293	287	288	291	301	309					
FY10 plan (2009)										287	n/a	n/a	n/a	n/a	n/a	n/a	n/a	n/a	n/a				
FY11 plan (2010)											284	287	287	285	285	292	298	305	311	315			
FY12 plan (2011)												290	287	286	286	297	301	311	316	322	324		
FY13 plan (2012)													285	285	279	276	284	285	292	300	295	296	298
FY14 plan (2013)														282	270	280	283	291	300	295	296	297	297

Source: Navy 30-year shipbuilding plans supplemented by annual Navy budget submissions (including 5-year shipbuilding plans) for fiscal years shown. **n/a** means not available—see notes below.

Notes: The FY2001 30-year plan submitted in 2000 was submitted under a one-time-only legislative provision, Section 1013 of the FY2000 National Defense Authorization Act (S. 1059/P.L. 106-65 of October 5, 1999). No provision required DOD to submit a 30-year shipbuilding plan in 2001 or 2002, when Congress considered DOD's proposed FY2002 and FY2003 DOD budgets. Section 1022 of the FY2003 Bob Stump National Defense Authorization Act (H.R. 4546/P.L. 107-314 of December 2, 2002) created a requirement to submit a 30-year shipbuilding plan each year, in conjunction with each year's defense budget. This provision was codified at

10 U.S.C. 231. The first 30-year plan submitted under this provision was the one submitted in 2003, in conjunction with the proposed FY2004 DOD budget. For the next several years, 30-year shipbuilding plans were submitted each year, in conjunction with each year's proposed DOD budget. An exception occurred in 2009, the first year of the Obama Administration, when DOD submitted a proposed budget for FY2010 with no accompanying FYDP or 30-year Navy shipbuilding plan. The FY2006 plan included data for only selected years beyond FY2011. Section 1023 of the FY2011 Ike Skelton National Defense Authorization Act (H.R. 6523/P.L. 111-383 of January 7, 2011) amended 10 U.S.C. 231 to require DOD to submit a 30-year shipbuilding plan once every four years, in the same year that DOD submits a Quadrennial Defense Review (QDR). Consistent with Section 1023, DOD did not submit a new 30-year shipbuilding plan at the time that it submitted the proposed FY2012 DOD budget. At the request of the House Armed Services Committee, the Navy submitted the FY2012 30-year (FY2012-FY2041) shipbuilding plan in late-May 2011. Section 1011 of the FY2012 National Defense Authorization Act (H.R. 1540/P.L. 112-81 of December 31, 2011) amended 10 U.S.C. 231 to reinstate the requirement to submit a 30-year shipbuilding plan each year, in conjunction with each year's defense budget.

Oversight Issues for Congress for FY2014

Impact of March 1, 2013, Sequester on FY2013 Funding

June 2013 DOD Report on March 1, 2013, Sequester

One issue for Congress concerns the impact on Navy shipbuilding programs of the March 1, 2013, sequester on FY2013 funding and unobligated prior-year funding. DOD's June 2013 report to Congress on the March 1, 2013, sequester states that the sequester reduced FY2013 and unobligated prior-year funding in the Navy's shipbuilding account (known formally as the Shipbuilding and Conversion, Navy, or SCN, appropriation account) by $1,752.7 million, or about 7.6%, including

- $541.2 million in the DDG-51 destroyer program;

- $492.3 million in the Virginia class attack submarine program;

- $184.2 million in the LCS program;

- $176.3 in the program for performing mid-life nuclear refueling overhauls (called refueling complex overhauls, or RCOHs) on existing Nimitz (CVN-68) class aircraft carriers;

- $74.5 million in the program for building new CVN-78 class aircraft carriers;

- $71.1 million for the LHA Replacement amphibious assault ship program;

- $70.3 million for the DDG-1000 destroyer program;

- $58.8 million in the LPD-17 amphibious ship program;

- $25.7 million for the Moored Training Ship (MTS) program to convert an older attack submarine into a moored training platform;

- $24.7 million for ship outfitting costs;

- $21.4 million for the JHSV program;

- $10.0 million for the LCAC SLEP (air cushioned landing craft service life extension program); and

- amounts of less than $1 million each from a few other SCN-funded programs.[5]

The first two items listed above account for $1,033.5 million, or about 59.0%, of the total amount sequestered from the SCN account. The first four items listed above account for $1,394.0 million, or about 79.5%, of the total amount sequestered from the SCN account.

The impact of the March 1, 2013, sequester on an individual Navy shipbuilding program will depend on the particular circumstances of that program, including, among other things, the impact

---

[5] *Department of Defense Report on the Joint Committee Sequestration for Fiscal Year 2013*, June 2013, pp. 36, 36A, 37, and 37A (pdf pages 85-88 of 438).

of the March 1, 2013, sequester on funding for research and development efforts supporting that program. CRS reports on individual shipbuilding programs provide additional details about the impact of the sequester on individual programs. (For a list of these reports, see "CRS Reports Tracking Legislation on Specific Navy Shipbuilding Programs" at the end of the "Legislative Activity for FY2014" section.)

Executability of Third DDG-51 Funded in FY2013

A key question regarding the impact of the sequester on FY2013 funding concerns the executability (i.e., on the Navy's ability to go ahead with the construction) of the third DDG-51 destroyer that was funded in FY2013. This ship is to be the 10th ship in a DDG-51 multiyear procurement (MYP) contract for FY2013-FY2017 that was awarded in early June 2013.

At a May 8, 2013, hearing on Navy shipbuilding programs before the Seapower subcommittee of the Senate Armed Services Committee, Sean Stackley, the Assistant Secretary of the Navy for Research, Development and Acquisition (i.e., the Navy's acquisition executive), testified that as a result of the March 1, 2013, sequester, there is an approximately $300 million funding shortfall in the DDG-51 program that creates a problem for executing the third DDG-51 that was funded in FY2013.[6] Stackley stated that the Navy is ready to work with Congress to address this issue, and that the ship is treated as an option in the DDG-51 MYP contract.[7]

The suggestion from the Navy's testimony is that if Congress were to address the funding shortfall for the DDG-51 program this year, either through its action on the Navy's proposed FY2014 budget or in some other way, the ship could be added to the MYP contract following the award of the contract by exercising the contract's option for the ship. If that were to happen this year, it would not substantially affect the schedule for building this ship, because the Navy from the start has anticipated building the ship on a schedule consistent with what would be expected for a ship funded in FY2014. In other words, for construction scheduling purposes, the Navy from the start has anticipated treating the ship like a "second FY2014 DDG-51" rather than a third FY2013 DDG-51.

November 7, 2013, Navy Testimony

At a November, 7, 2013, hearing before the Senate Armed Services Committee on the impact of sequestration on the national defense, Admiral Jonathan Greenert testified, in a statement similar to the one he used at the September 18, 2013, hearing discussed below, that

> Looking at the nearer term, the FY 2013 sequestration reductions compelled us to reduce our afloat and ashore operations and created a significant shore maintenance backlog. However, the effects were barely manageable because we received authorization to reprogram funds into appropriate maintenance accounts, and we were able to use prior-year investment balances to mitigate reductions to investment programs. Impact to Navy programs, caused by the combination of a continuing resolution and sequestration, included:

---

[6] Transcript of hearing. Stackley testified that the sequester created an approximately $560 million funding shortfall in the DDG-51 program (as mentioned earlier DOD's June 2013 report provided a final figure of $541.2 million), and that the Navy was able to identify about $260 million in funding offsets to apply to the shortfall, leaving a shortfall of about $300 million.

[7] Transcript of hearing.

• Cancelled five ship deployments.

• Delayed deployment of USS HARRY S TRUMAN strike group by six months.

• Planned inactivation, instead of repairing, USS MIAMI due to rising cost and inadequate maintenance funds.

• Reduced facilities restoration and modernization by about 30%.

• Furloughed DON civilian employees for 6 days, which, combined with a hiring freeze, reduced our maintenance and sustainment capacity by taking away logisticians, comptrollers, engineers, contracting officers, and planners.

• Reduced base operations, including port and airfield operations, by about 20%.

• Cancelled the Blue Angels' season and most non-essential port visits for Fleet Weeks.[8]

October 23, 2013, Navy Testimony

At an October 23, 2013, hearing before the Tactical Air and Land Forces subcommittee of the House Armed Services Committee on the impacts of a continuing resolution (CR) and sequestration on acquisition and modernization, Department of the Navy officials testified that

> ... FY 2013 sequestration reduced the DON top-line by approximately $11 billion and impacted our readiness, operations and procurement. The effects were addressed by curtailing operations, deferring maintenance, depleting unobligated prior-year balances in our investment accounts, deferring costs to future year budgets, and employing the limited transfer authority provided to the DON. These measures which mitigated the immediate impacts were insufficient to bear the full weight of sequestration, resulting in delays to development schedules and reductions to procurement quantities. The net effects of these deferrals, delays, and program cuts are added bills and increased costs in FY 2014 and beyond.

> In support of our warfighters, the DON prioritized readiness for deployed and next to deploy forces. By this action, the Navy and Marine Corps were able to preserve the capability and capacity to meet the highest priority Combatant Commander demands, including crisis response and theater security cooperation, although participation levels were reduced in some cases. However, coupled with the continuing resolution for the first six months of FY 2013, sequestration compelled us to reduce our operations, including cancelling five ship deployments, delaying deployment of the USS HARRY S TRUMAN strike group by six months, and creating a significant maintenance backlog that has carried over into FY 2014. The Navy was forced to defer required maintenance on 16 airframes and 55 engines/engine modules and reduce non-deployed flying hours, thereby jeopardizing planned aircraft modernization, mission system software capability improvements, fatigue-life management, depot support, and the flight-hour program which maintains pilot proficiency and readiness. While this preserved forward deployed activities and training for next-to-deploy forces, it increased risk in the readiness of our non-deployed units which will take years to recover.

---

[8] Statement of Admiral Jonathan Greenert, U.S. Navy, Chief of Naval Operations, Before the Senate Armed Services Committee on the Impact of Sequestration on the National Defense, November 7, 2013, pp. 11-12.

Sequestration also resulted in the furlough of DON civilian employees for six days, which when combined with a hiring freeze, reduced our maintenance and sustainment capacity by taking away logisticians, comptrollers, engineers, contracting officers, and planners. Navy facilities sustainment, restoration and modernization was reduced by approximately 30% and base operations, including port and airfield operations, was reduced by approximately 20%.[9]

September 18, 2013, Navy Testimony

At a September 18, 2013, hearing before the House Armed Services Committee on planning for sequestration in FY2014 and perspectives of the military services on the Strategic Choices and Management Review (SCMR), Admiral Jonathan Greenert, the Chief of Naval Operations (CNO) testified, in a statement similar to the one he used at the November 7, 2013, hearing discussed above, that

> the FY 2013 sequestration reductions compelled us to reduce our afloat and ashore operations and created a significant afloat and ashore maintenance backlog. However, the effects were barely manageable due to authorization to reprogram funds into appropriate maintenance accounts, and we were able to use prior-year investment balances to mitigate reductions to investment programs. Impact to Navy programs, caused by the combination of a continuing resolution and sequestration, included:
>
> • Cancelled five ship deployments.
>
> • Delayed deployment of [the aircraft carrier] USS HARRY S TRUMAN strike group by six months.
>
> • Planned inactivation, instead of repairing, [the attack submarine] USS MIAMI due to rising cost and inadequate maintenance funds.
>
> • Reduced facilities restoration and modernization by about 30%.
>
> • Furloughed DON [Department of the Navy] civilian employees for 6 days, which, combined with a hiring freeze, reduced our maintenance and sustainment capacity by taking away logisticians, comptrollers, engineers, contracting officers, and planners.
>
> • Reduced base operations, including port and airfield operations, by about 20%.
>
> • Cancelled the Blue Angels' season and most non-essential port visits for Fleet Weeks.[10]

---

[9] Statement of Hon. Sean J. Stackley, Assistant Secretary of the Navy (Research, Development and Acquisition), and Vice Admiral Allen G. Myers, USN, Deputy Chief of Naval Operations, Integration of Capabilities and Resources, and Lieutenant General Glenn M. Walters, USMC, Deputy Commandant for Programs and Resources, Before the Tactical Air and Land Forces Subcommittee of the House Armed Services Committee on Impacts of a Continuing Resolution and Sequestration on Department of the Navy Acquisition, Programming & Industrial Base, October 23, 2013, pp. 2-3.

[10] Statement of Admiral Jonathan Greenert, U.S. Navy, Chief of Naval Operations, Before the House Armed Services Committee on Planning for Sequestration in FY 2014 and Perspectives of the Military Services on the Strategic Choices and Management Review, September 18, 2013, pp. 2-3

September 5, 2013, CNO Remarks

At a September 5, 2013, event at the American Enterprise Institute (AEI), Admiral Jonathan Greenert, stated that

> ...we have 285 ships today, about an average of 95 [of those ships] deployed. This is about a 90 day average. ... But we're about 10 [ships] down in this deployment piece. I.e., we were about 105 deployed [ships] about a year ago, and that is a factor of this last year of the budget limitations that we've had....
>
> This rebalance to the Asia Pacific, despite operations around the world, despite Mideast operations, continues. It has slowed down. The continuing resolution of '13 and sequestration has slowed us down but it's moving ahead....
>
> The effect of sequestration, the continuing resolution in FY13 pretty much came about as we predicted and as we testified to. The budget reduction was about $11 billion to us, to the Navy. And we were fortunate enough to reach back to prior year money, which hadn't been fully obligated, and pull that forward into '13 and it helped mitigate that. That's a one-time operation that we were able to do.
>
> We in fact had to cancel five ship deployments in FY13. [And regarding] Our surge capacity, the ability to respond here [indicating an overseas location on a briefing slide]. [using] Those ships that are back here in the continental U.S. Usually we have three carrier strike groups and three amphibious ready groups able to respond within a week. We have one [of each] now. That's going to be the story in FY14 as we look ahead. So it's a reduction in surge [capacity]. That's where a lot of the, if you will, the reductions in the budget kind of manifested themselves.
>
> We've done very little shore maintenance upgrades. If there's an area that I'm concerned about and I have to watch closely, it is our shore readiness. This is where we're taking a lot of the reductions and we've got to be careful of that.[11]

August 1, 2013, Navy Testimony

At an August 1, 2013, hearing before the Seapower and Projection Forces subcommittee and the Readiness subcommittee of the House Armed Services Committee on Navy surface ship maintenance and readiness, the Navy testified:

Current readiness

> The combination of the continuing resolution and sequestration put twenty three FY13 surface ship availabilities at risk, and represented the most immediate threat to surface ship readiness. We were able to restore all but eight availabilities when the FY13 appropriations bill was passed, and we appreciate the support of Congress on a reprogramming which will fund the last eight availabilities.
>
> The FY13 appropriations bill with sequestration left the Navy with a $4.1 billion shortfall in our Operations and Maintenance (O&MN) accounts compared with the President's 2013

---

[11] Transcript of remarks by Admiral Jonathan Greenert, Chief of Naval Operations, at the American Enterprise Institute (AEI), September 5, 2013, on American Military Strategy In A Time of Declining Budgets, provided to CRS by Navy Office of Legislative Affairs, September 6, 2013.

budget submission. This has had an impact on Fleet operations and readiness in FY13, and will carry over into FY14. Specifically, it has degraded our ability to provide the level of global presence and surge capacity that we have executed over the last several years.

The decreased presence is apparent in our reduction of deployed carrier strike groups, as well as a reduction in Southern Command and European Command deployments. For example, of the ten vessels scheduled to conduct deployments to Southern Command this fiscal year, only three will complete their deployments as planned. We will continue to provide ready forces to execute the highest priority deployments, providing the Combatant Commanders with the presence and capabilities they need most to execute the Defense Strategic Guidance. However, reduction of presence or elimination of deployments to any region is noticed by both our allies and potential adversaries, degrading not only our ability to build and foster cooperative relationships with our maritime partners, but also reducing our capability to ensure operational access and freedom of action. You cannot surge trust; rather you have to be there, building it every day.

The decrease in our surge capacity is less apparent than reduced presence, but it still causes great concern due to the impact on war plans and contingency operations. The net effect is that surging our remaining surge capacity will likely lead to gaps in future regularly scheduled presence operations. Due to fiscal constraints, the Navy has been forced to prioritize maintenance and training for those forces deploying in FY14. Thus, those forces deploying after FY14 will receive reduced maintenance and training, decreasing our ability to surge these forces in case of emergency. This shortfall in surge capacity will be problematic if our forces are required to respond to contingencies. Currently, our surge forces are restricted to the forces trained and equipped for the next deployment, while the rest of the Fleet is in a training and material readiness status below "ready to deploy in all warfare areas."[12]

July 19, 2013, Navy Press Briefing

At a July 19, 2013, press briefing, Admiral Jonathan Greenert, the Chief of Naval Operations, stated that

So could I get the Navy slide today up there, please? Thank you. I think you have this as part of the handout, but this is where your Navy is today. Presence remains our mandate. This is what we're mostly about. And it's a central element of our defense strategic guidance.

As you can see, we have about 95 ships deployed, and about 3,700 operational aircraft are also out there. I'll tell you, since sequestration sort of set in with the impact of a continuing resolution, we're down about 10 ships from, say, about a year ago or actually several months ago, forward deployed. So there is an impact....

In the Southern Command, sequestration has effectively caused us to reduce our combatant ships to zero. You can see up there [on the slide]. I tell you, there are other naval forces in the region, non-combatant ships and other forces, but we're zero [ships] today [in the Southern Command area]. And that was a deliberate decision approved by the Secretary of Defense as part of our global force management operation.

---

[12] Statement of Rear Admiral Thomas Rowden, Director, Surface Warfare (N96) and Rear Admiral Timothy Matthews, Director, Fleet Readiness (N43) on Ensuring Navy Surface Force Effectiveness With limited Maintenance Resources before the House Armed Services Committee Subcommittee on Seapower and Projection Forces and Subcommittee on Readiness, August 1, 2013, pp. 1-2.

I would tell you, it'll undulate a little bit somewhere around zero, one or two as we go through the process....

So a little bit on the—the budget and sequestration, it's on my mind daily, and the fiscal year '13 appropriation bill helped us quite a bit. We're out there today with one carrier strike group and one amphibious ready group deployed to each theater, so we've got one in the Arabian Gulf region and one in the Western Pacific of each. But the issue is, the backup— that would be the surge force—we're not where we need to be in that regard. We have today one carrier strike group and one amphibious ready group ready to deploy with all the capabilities that we have in our covenant to our combatant commanders. The rest of the fleet is not ready to deploy with all the capabilities that are needed that we would normally have in our fleet response plan, and that's really the issue that we have there.

A year ago, I would tell you, we had three carrier strike groups and three amphibious ready groups ready to surge. And if there were a contingency, we had to take on a large operation, the surge force would be a concern, and the concern would be the capabilities that we would bring and whether or not they were the right capabilities.

It may not be readily apparent to many, because as you look out there, you say, hey, it kind of looks the same out there. But it's—it's the surge issue, and it's a real issue.

Now, for the remainder of the year, this year, this fiscal year, we'll be adjusting our operations and maintenance spending to meet, really, the FY [fiscal year] '14 deployments. The kids are training and doing maintenance this year for next year's deployments. And we have a plan in place, working with the Congress on a reprogramming, to restore the maintenance availabilities that we had set aside due to our budgetary issues earlier in the year. And we're trying to maintain as much of our training operations as feasible, for the reasons I've said before.

My real concern tends to be the shore facilities and the shore readiness. They're taking the brunt of this reduction here in '13, both in the case of the continuing resolution and sequestration. And I'm looking very closely at this. We are effectively doing no projects, no restoration or modernization projects, and we have taken our base operations and our sustainment, the very basic things, down to really the minimum that we think is safe and appropriate.[13]

May 8, 2013, Navy Testimony

The Navy's prepared statement for the May 8, 2013, hearing on Navy shipbuilding programs before the Seapower subcommittee of the Senate Armed Services Committee stated the following regarding the impact of the March 1, 2013, sequester:

Sequestration ... reduced the Fiscal Year 2013 funding across all [Navy] accounts by roughly 8 percent, or about $10.7 billion total, thus directly impacting current and future readiness. The Navy is still reconciling the impact of this reduction; however, due to the mechanics of its implementation and the limits on Department-wide transfer authority authorized by the Fiscal Year 2013 Defense Appropriations Act, it is likely that the Department [of the Navy] will be compelled to reduce our near term forward presence, our planned depot maintenance

---

[13] Department of Defense Press Briefing by Adm. Greenert in the Pentagon Briefing Room, July 19, 2013, accessed August 7, 2013, at http://www.defense.gov/transcripts/transcript.aspx?transcriptid=5278. The term "fiscal year" appears in brackets in the original.

and training to support future operational rotations, our procurement of ships, aircraft and weapons systems to meet our force structure and inventory requirements, and our investment in future capabilities and readiness; thus impacting our future readiness. Every major weapon system is impacted by sequestration in 2013 with impacts ranging from reducing quantities procured, delaying schedules (delivery and initial operational capability), deferring costs to future years (particularly in the case of executing programs, such as shipbuilding), and absorbing cost growth due to all of these impacts.[14]

During the discussion portion of the hearing, Sean Stackley, the Assistant Secretary of the Navy for Research, Development and Acquisition (i.e., the Navy's acquisition executive), made additional comments regarding the impact of the March 1, 2013, sequester in response to questions. Early in the discussion portion of the hearing, he stated:

> Let me start by just describing 2013 since we're dealing with sequestration in the current budget year.
>
> As I described at the outset, each of the program lines was impacted by sequestration. So in 2013, we are working line by line to mitigate the impact by either paying for the sequestration impact to prior year assets, which we had accumulated through the last four to five years of shipbuilding or trying to defer certain costs that we can defer to a later point in the cycle in order to keep the plan procurement on track. And there are certain cases where we're looking at do we need to de-scope certain items on the shipbuilding plan, but trying to keep the overall force structure number healthy.
>
> In that approach, in fact, the [third] DDG 51 that was added by Congress in 2013 is, in fact, held up. Otherwise, the balance of the shipbuilding program is going forward admittedly at some risk, so some increased risk in terms of called budget executability. So we're trying to do this very mindfully if we allow sequestration to stop us in our tracks that will simply cause or cause the disruption to go through the roof.
>
> So we're going to continue to work that destroyer with Congress so that you all understand its specific impact. We're going to continue to execute the balance of the shipbuilding program in '13.
>
> We have brought forward the budget request in '14, which as you're well aware does not account for a sequestration in '14. And, in fact, in '14 and out in a more strategic review that's been accomplished under the direction and guidance of the secretary of Defense, we are looking at shipbuilding amidst all of the capabilities that the department is pursuing in terms of what are the impacts associated with reduction of the top line, and then what are the priorities that we need to bring forward in terms of funding those capabilities.
>
> And central to all of that is driving down the cost of what we're procuring and driving out the cost of our doing business so that more of the dollars available can go towards capability.[15]

Later in the hearing, he stated that

---

[14] Statement of The Honorable Sean J. Stackley, Assistant Secretary of the Navy (Research, Development and Acquisition) and Vice Admiral Allen G. Myers, Deputy Chief of Naval Operations for Integration of Capabilities and Resources and Vice Admiral Kevin M. McCoy, Commander, Naval Sea Systems Command, Before the Subcommittee on Seapower of the Senate Armed Services Committee on Department of the Navy Shipbuilding Programs, May 8, 2013, p. 5.

[15] Transcript of hearing.

across the board, sequestration affects everything that we do. So first, it has created a great deal of uncertainty in terms of our planning and allowing us to prioritize within a top line where our investments will go, so uncertainty creates an impact.

That uncertainty then trickles down into planning and procurement in the vendor base—first year [sic: tier] shipyards and then down in the vendor base below that. So we're having to keep an eye on ensuring that the vendor base that we're relying on in a longer term to support our shipbuilding requirements doesn't break as a result of delays or uncertainty from sequestration.

And then the most poignant impact is the dollar impact directly. Everything that we've been doing to try to reduce the cost of our shipbuilding program whether it's stabilizing requirements, whether it's trying to get stable production rates that allow investment by the shipbuilders, trying to wrap in a multiyear where we harvest the significant savings, putting that inside of a fixed price contract where we have confidence in the savings, sequestration unravels that to an extent.

So now what we have to do when we look at—prospectively at sequestration on the outyear budgets, we've got to fight for the priority that shipbuilding demands in order to hit the CNO's [Chief of Naval Operation's] requirement within the budget so that our efforts to reduce cost don't, in fact, go in a reverse direction as a result of sequestration and we end up with potential disruption, taking low shipbuilding rates that we have today and driving them lower and then ultimately driving those costs up. So we have to avoid that spiral that could occur if we unravel what we've been attempting to do with regards to stabilizing the shipbuilding plan over the last several years.[16]

Potential Impact of Possible Late 2013/Early 2014 Sequester on FY2014 Funding

Another potential issue for Congress concerns the potential impact on Navy shipbuilding programs of a possible sequester on FY2014 funding and unobligated prior-year funding) that might occur in late 2013 or early 2014 under the terms of the Budget Control Act of 2011 (S. 365/P.L. 112-25 of August 2, 2011).

November 7, 2013, Navy Testimony

At a November, 7, 2013, hearing before the Senate Armed Services Committee on the impact of sequestration on the national defense, Admiral Jonathan Greenert testified, in a statement similar to the one he used at the September 18, 2013, hearing discussed below, that

> Sequestration in FY 2014, particularly if combined with restrictions of a continuing resolution (CR), will reduce our readiness in the near-term and in the long-term exacerbate program impacts from budget reductions required under current law. The impacts below assume an approximate 10% cut to the Navy's budget; however, with military personnel accounts exempted, the cut could increase to 14% in all other appropriations. In addition, the restrictions imposed by a CR will reduce our ability to manage the impact of sequestration. The impacts of this reduced funding will be realized in two main categories of budget accounts: (1) operations and maintenance and (2) investments.

---

[16] Transcript of hearing.

(1) Operation and maintenance accounts will absorb a larger reduction than in FY 2013 from a smaller overall amount of money; in addition we must begin to address deferred "carry over" bills from FY 2013 that total approximately $2.3 billion over the next five years. Because we will prioritize meeting current presence requirements, we will be able to preserve 95% of the forward presence originally directed under the FY 2014 Global Force Management Allocation Plan (GFMAP). However, this is still only about half of the Combatant Commander's original request. To ensure adequate funding for the most important deployments, we were compelled to adjust the plan in advance of FY 2014 to remove the deployment of one CG to the Middle East, two salvage ships to Africa and South America and five large surface combatants to the Western Pacific. Most concerning, however, we will have two thirds less surge capacity in FY2014. Our planned presence to meet the GFMAP in FY 2015 and beyond will also be at risk because maintenance cancelled in FY2014 may result in ships being unable to deploy in future years. At a minimum this lost maintenance will reduce the service life of these ships.

Because of the mechanics of sequestration, we cannot reprogram (move) funds from other accounts into operations and maintenance to make up for the sequestered amount. As a result, within operations and maintenance, we have to "go where the money is" and find savings in training, maintenance, civilian personnel, and shore facilities. The reductions in fleet training we are compelled to make will result in only one non-deployed CSG and one ARG trained and ready for surge operations – notionally without these reductions there would be three of each ready to deploy within about two weeks.

We will be compelled to cancel or defer planned FY 2014 fleet maintenance, including 34 of 55 surface ship maintenance periods totaling about $950 million – all in private shipyards – and 191 of about 700 aircraft depot maintenance actions. This missed maintenance will inevitably take time off the expected service life of our ships and aircraft, which in turn will make it harder to sustain even the smaller fleet we will have if the BCA caps remain in place for the long term. For example, a recent Center for Naval Analysis study estimated cancelling and not making up one maintenance period at the ten-year point in a DDG's life will shorten its overall service life by about five years.

We will be compelled to keep in place our freeze on hiring for most civilian positions. Ashore we will continue to conduct only safety-essential renovation and modernization of facilities, further increasing the large backlog in that area.

(2) Investment accounts will be particularly impacted by sequestration in FY 2014, and we will not be able to use prior-year funds to mitigate shortfalls as we did in FY 2013. Without Congressional action or mitigating circumstances, the reductions imposed by sequestration and the limitations of a CR will compel us to:

• Cancel planned FY 2014 procurement of an SSN, an LCS and an AFSB; also, delay an SSN planned for FY 2015 procurement. Each of these would further worsen the reduction in fleet size, described earlier in this statement, that the BCA would compel us to make over the long term.

• Delay the planned start of construction on the first SSBN(X) from FY 2021 to FY 2022. This would cause us to be unable to meet U.S. Strategic Command presence requirements when the Ohio-class SSBN retires.

• Cancel procurement of 11 tactical aircraft (4 EA-18G Growler, 1 F-35C Lightning II, 1 E-2D Advanced Hawkeye, 2 P-8A Poseidon, 3 MH-60 Seahawk) and about 400 weapons, exacerbating future BCA-driven reductions in our capabilities to project power despite A2/AD threats.

• Delay delivery of USS GERALD R. FORD (CVN-78) by two years, extending the period of 10 CVN in service, and lowering surge capacity.

• Delay the mid-life overhaul of USS GEORGE WASHINGTON (CVN 73) scheduled for FY 2016, disrupting today's "heel-to-toe" CVN overhaul schedule and reducing near-term CVN capacity.

In order to avoid or remedy some of the FY 2014 impacts described above, we need Congress to approve authorization and appropriations bills. This would enable the Navy to transfer funds, pursue innovative acquisition approaches, start new projects, increase production quantities, and complete ships. This would:

• Keep SSBN(X) on schedule to sustain required SSBN capacity after the Ohio class begins to retire.

• Buy two Virginia class SSN in FY 2014 as planned and keep FY 2015 SSN procurement on schedule. These actions will help maintain our undersea dominance and ability to project power despite A2/AD threats.

• Protect CVN-73's mid-life overhaul and complete CVN-78 on time to sustain CVN capacity.

• Build the planned AFSB in FY 2014, which is needed to meet DSG and combatant commander presence requirements for CT/IW capability.

• Restore half of the cancelled surface ship maintenance availabilities to protect FY 2015 presence.[17]

October 23, 2013, Navy Testimony

At an October 23, 2013, hearing before the Tactical Air and Land Forces subcommittee of the House Armed Services Committee on the impacts of a continuing resolution (CR) and sequestration on acquisition and modernization, Department of the Navy officials testified that

> the effect of another continuing resolution and sequestration-level reductions in FY 2014 would compound the impacts of the FY 2013 CR/sequestration. Operating under a CR in FY 2014, with corresponding restrictions on program funding and execution, significantly impairs our ability to effectively allocate resources and meet mission requirements. Compounding a CR with reductions to the FY 2014 budget in accordance with the mechanics of sequestration would remove from the Department its ability to provide warfighting capability and capacity with the measures of efficiency essential to balancing the requirements of the Defense Strategic Guidance with the fiscal constraints of the Budget Control Act (BCA) of 2011.
>
> In the near-term, the Navy and Marine Corps will prioritize preserving the global presence requirements set forth in the FY 2014 Global Force Management Allocation Plan (GFMAP). However, under sequestration-level funding, we will have less surge capability and our planned presence for FY 2015 and beyond will be at risk. Sequestration will compel us to forfeit long-term priorities to fund near-term readiness; resourcing training and maintenance

[17] Statement of Admiral Jonathan Greenert, U.S. Navy, Chief of Naval Operations, Before the Senate Armed Services Committee on the Impact of Sequestration on the National Defense, November 7, 2013, pp. 12-14.

of the next to deploy at the expense of those who will follow. Meanwhile, across the board reductions to investment accounts will slow production on factory floors across the defense industrial base adding cost and schedule to today's weapon systems; and equally critical, these reductions will drive delay into the development of those leading edge weapon systems that provide our warfighters with the asymmetric advantage they hold over our adversaries....

The effects of an FY2014 CR and sequestration take away from the Department its ability to provide warfighting capability and capacity with the measures of efficiency essential to balancing the requirements of the Defense Strategic Guidance with the fiscal constraints under current law. Without Congress acting to change the current path, our warfighters will have less surge capability and our long-term priorities will be traded off to fund near-term readiness. Further, weapon system development timelines will be extended and costs will be higher, production unit costs will increase, and the risk to the long-term viability of the defense industrial base will increase.

Our appeal is that Congress complete its work on the FY 2014 defense authorization and appropriations bills and eliminate sequestration before we are driven to irreversible actions which impair our collective responsibility to provide for the nation's defense.

We understand the importance of resolving our fiscal challenges to ensure our nation's security and future prosperity and look forward to working with Congress to ensure our Navy and Marine Corps remain the world's preeminent maritime and expeditionary force.[18]

Regarding naval aviation programs in particular, the Department of the Navy officials testified at the hearing that

Our FY 2014 Naval Aviation Budget request prioritizes several central themes: 5th generation fighter/attack capability; persistent multi-role intelligence, surveillance, and reconnaissance; supporting capabilities of electronic attack, maritime patrol, and vertical lift; robust strike weapons programs; and targeted modernization of the force for relevance and sustainability. It enables Naval Aviation to continue recapitalization of our aging fleets of airborne early warning, maritime patrol, electronic attack, and vertical lift platforms.

FY 2014 sequestration is estimated to impose approximately a 10% cut to the DONs top-line budget. With military personnel exempted by the President, the reduction increases approximately to 14% in all other appropriations. With this loss of obligational authority, no use of prior year investment funds to mitigate shortfalls, and a need to address deferred FY 2013 carry over bills, all aspects of Naval Aviation will be negatively impacted, including both current readiness and development of future capabilities, eroding our margin of military superiority.

A FY 2014 CR further creates several impacts, becoming more serious the longer the CR continues into the fiscal year. Under a CR, we are unable to use funds for new procurements or increase production rates above those sustained in FY 2013. Major programs that will be affected include: F-35 Joint Strike Fighter (JSF), MQ-8 FireScout, EA-18G Growler, Joint Precision Approach and Landing System (JPALS), and Advanced Precision Kill Weapon System (APKWS II) integration with MH-60R Seahawk. The CR also prohibits new multi-

---

[18] Statement of Hon. Sean J. Stackley, Assistant Secretary of the Navy (Research, Development and Acquisition), and Vice Admiral Allen G. Myers, USN, Deputy Chief of Naval Operations, Integration of Capabilities and Resources, and Lieutenant General Glenn M. Walters, USMC, Deputy Commandant for Programs and Resources, Before the Tactical Air and Land Forces Subcommittee of the House Armed Services Committee on Impacts of a Continuing Resolution and Sequestration on Department of the Navy Acquisition, Programming & Industrial Base, October 23, 2013, pp. 1-2, 12.

year procurement contracts planned for the C-130J and E-2D aircraft and associated mission equipment, delaying awards to industry and impacting production lines, delivery schedules, and most importantly, additional cost levied on pressurized budgets.

Operation & Support (O&S) Impacts:

Maintenance is critical to ensure our aircraft meet their expected service lives, keep strike fighter inventories at required readiness, and to preclude a strike fighter inventory shortfall above manageable levels. Our FY 2014 President's Budget submission included the resources necessary to continue Service Life Extension Program (SLEP) efforts and modifications on legacy F/A-18A-D Hornets to extend their service lives from 6,000 flight hours to 10,000 flight hours. Sequestration, however, will require us to cancel or defer approximately 200 of 700 aircraft and 580 engine planned depot maintenance events; eroding the service life of the aircraft and making it more difficult to sustain even the smaller fleet we will have if the reduced discretionary funding caps remain in place. If the current law levels remain long term, the maintenance backlog will continue to compound, eventually leaving Navy with insufficient aircraft available in inventory to meet deployment and training readiness objectives.

Marine Corps aviation readiness will degrade with reductions to the flying hour program and depot maintenance in 2014. In 2013, approximately 70% of Marine squadrons met minimum deployable combat readiness. By 2015, we project this number will be reduced to approximately 60% as a result of sequestration.

Marine F/A-18A-D Hornet squadrons face the biggest challenge with regards to funding reductions and depot maintenance backlogs. In September 2013, approximately half of the available F/A-18 inventory was in an "out of reporting" status. This results in non-deployed squadrons having only seven aircraft available for tasking when the squadron requirement is 12 aircraft. It is estimated that by January 2015 that number will be reduced to four aircraft available per non-deployed F/A-18A-D squadron.

Personnel Impacts:

The DON relies on a 'total force' of military (active and reserve) and civilian personnel to execute its mission. Even with the exemption of military personnel accounts from sequestration in FY 2014, the DON will continue to drawdown military end strength as noted in the FY 2014 President's Budget Request. However, if the reduced discretionary caps continue in force past 2014, we will not be able to afford our planned force structure, putting the nation's ability to respond to crisis around the globe at risk.

The impacts to our civilian workforce will affect every state and be detrimental to the employees, their families, the DON mission, and local economies. While we will make every effort to protect civilians from another furlough in FY 2014, sequestration-level funding forces us to consider all civilian force shaping tools, to include Voluntary Separation Incentive Pay, Voluntary Early Retirement Authority, Reductions in Force (RIF), continued hiring restrictions, and reductions or eliminations of bonuses. With the direct loss of labor-hours, the workforce impacts also lead to inefficiencies caused by loss of learning, productivity losses, cost increases driven by lengthening schedules, increased burdens on military personnel, and lower morale – all of which translate to reduced readiness.

Investment Account Impacts:

Due to the mechanics of its implementation and the limits on Department-wide transfer authority, sequestration will again impact every program and system, forcing reductions in procurement quantities, delays in schedules (delivery and initial operational capability), deferral of costs to future years, and unnecessary cost growth.

The DON remains firmly committed to the JSF program as an essential platform in our immediate and long-range Navy and Marine Corps aviation strategy and the nation's security. However, these funding constraints would compel us to reduce aircraft procurement by one F-35B Short Take-Off and Vertical Landing variant and one F-35C Carrier Variant and delay JSF Block IIIF development, test, and evaluation flights resulting in increased risk of meeting planned initial operating capability dates. As we carefully monitor strike fighter inventory requirements and projected availability, these reductions and delays also add increased risk to our ability to meet operational demands for expeditionary strike and maintain a complementary mix of strike fighter aircraft.

Sequestration will compel us to reduce E/A-18G Growler procurement by up to four aircraft in FY 2014, relative to the budget request, which will decrease attrition reserve aircraft set aside for the Navy's expeditionary force. Although this reduction will not delay the transition from EA-6B Prowlers to EA-18G Growlers, it will increase the risk associated with inventory requirements to offset loss of aircraft over the life of the EA-18G. For more than half a century, the DON has been the leader in Airborne Electronic Attack (AEA) and this asymmetric naval capability remains in high demand by the joint force. This reduction would limit our only tactical AEA capability and reduce our ability to rapidly respond to emergent operations on short notice. With FY 2014 as the last year of production, there will be no opportunity to adjust in the future.

E-2D Advanced Hawkeye procurement will be reduced by one aircraft relative to the request in FY 2014. If the current law caps remain long-term, Navy would continue to field the Navy Integrated Fire Control – Counter Air (NIFC-CA) network with E-2D in 2015, but may have to reduce the number of CVWs that have this capability in 2020 from six in our FY 2014 President's Budget submission to four. The completion of transition to the E-2D would delay by three years from 2023 to 2026.

P-8A Poseidon procurement may be reduced by up to two aircraft in FY 2014. If the current law caps remain long-term, one potential scenario would not allow our development of capabilities to project power to stay ahead of potential adversaries' Anti-Access/Area Denial (A2/AD) capabilities, as our undersea capabilities will be slowed. For example, attainment of the required P-8A inventory (117) will be delayed from 2019 to 2020, and the completion of the transition from the P-3C to the P-8A will be delayed from 2019 to 2020. This would also increase the sustainment cost of supporting legacy P-3C aircraft.

MV-22B Osprey procurement will be reduced by up to three aircraft if sequestered in FY 2014. This action would threaten the V-22 Multi-Year Procurement (MYP) contract and require price renegotiation for all remaining aircraft. This significantly reduces the estimated $1 billion in cost savings over the span of the current MYP contract. The increase in unit costs will further reduce the quantity of aircraft that the Marine Corps can afford to purchase, delaying full stand-up of future MV-22 squadrons, and Full Operational Capability.

Sequestration-level funding will also force reductions and delays in Unmanned Aerial Systems (UAS) programs. The Marine Corps will be required to reduce RQ-21 Small Tactical Unmanned Air Systems (STUAS) procurement by one system, resulting in a production rate below its minimum sustainment rate and increased system cost. This will put the program at risk, eliminating a critical capability for persistent ship and land-based ISR support for tactical-level maneuver decisions and unit level force defense and force protection missions. The MQ-4C Triton UAS (formerly known as BAMS for Broad Area Maritime Surveillance) initial operational test and evaluation will be delayed up to 12 months, delaying the persistent maritime intelligence, surveillance, and reconnaissance coverage it will provide to increase our maritime domain awareness and presence.

Overall, relative to the Budget request, sequestration in FY 2014 would result in the loss of an estimated 25 aircraft (2 F-35, 4 EA-18G, 3 MV-22, 4 H-1, 1 E-2D, 2 P-8A, 1 KC-130J, 3 MH-60, 1 UC-12, and 4 JPATS) across the Navy and Marine Corps and the loss of multi-year procurement contract savings. Critical development and delivery of capabilities will be delayed, putting our warfighters in increased risk against technologically advanced adversaries, especially over the long-term.

Sequestration delays fielding critical capabilities, breaks multi-year procurements, and reduces the quantity of strike and ship self-defense weapons. A broad spectrum of key strike weapons would be reduced, to include as many as seventy-three Joint Standoff Weapons; forty-six Tomahawk cruise missiles; fifty-one Hellfire weapons; forty-two Advanced Anti-Radiation Guided Missiles; and thirty-four AIM-9X Sidewinder missiles; thereby reducing our overall strike capability and capacity. We would also be required to make cuts in ammunition and training munitions that would be below minimum inventory requirements thereby placing Fleet training and readiness at further risk. These cuts would affect General Purpose Bombs, Practice Bombs, Air Expendable Countermeasures, Airborne Rockets, and Cartridge Actuated Devices/Propellant Actuated Devices.

If current law level caps continue, we would also see key components of the planned improved air-to-air infrared kill (IR) chain that circumvents adversary radar jamming, delayed by two years and the new, longer range AIM-9X/Block III missile delayed by up to two years. Improvements to the air-to-air radio frequency (RF) kill chain also would be slowed down as F/A-18E/F Block II Super Hornet anti-jamming upgrades would be delayed to 2020 and the equipping of all Pacific carrier air wings with the medium-range AIM-120D missile delayed by two years to 2022.[19]

September 18, 2013, Navy Testimony

At a September 18, 2013, hearing before the House Armed Services Committee on planning for sequestration in FY2014 and perspectives of the military services on the Strategic Choices and Management Review (SCMR), Admiral Jonathan Greenert testified, in a statement similar to the one he used at the November 7, 2013, hearing discussed above, that

Sequestration in FY 2014, particularly if combined with restrictions of a continuing resolution (CR), will reduce our readiness in the near-term and exacerbate program impacts from budget reductions required under current law in the long-term. The impacts below assume an approximate 10% cut to the Navy's budget; however, with military personnel accounts exempted, the cut could increase to 14% in all other appropriations. In addition, the restrictions imposed by a CR will reduce our ability to manage the impact of sequestration. The impacts of this reduced funding will be realized in two main categories of budget accounts: (1) operations and maintenance and (2) investments.

(1) Operation and maintenance accounts, if sequestered under a CR, will absorb a larger reduction than in FY 2013 from a smaller amount; in addition we must begin to address

---

[19] Statement of Hon. Sean J. Stackley, Assistant Secretary of the Navy (Research, Development and Acquisition), and Vice Admiral Allen G. Myers, USN, Deputy Chief of Naval Operations, Integration of Capabilities and Resources, and Lieutenant General Glenn M. Walters, USMC, Deputy Commandant for Programs and Resources, Before the Tactical Air and Land Forces Subcommittee of the House Armed Services Committee on Impacts of a Continuing Resolution and Sequestration on Department of the Navy Acquisition, Programming & Industrial Base, October 23, 2013, pp. 3-8.

deferred "carry over" bills from FY 2013 that total approximately $2.3 billion over the next five years. Because we will prioritize meeting current presence requirements, we will be able to preserve 95% of the forward presence originally directed under the FY 2014 Global Force Management Allocation Plan (GFMAP). However, this is only about half of the Combatant Commander's original request. To ensure adequate funding for the most important deployments, we were compelled to adjust the plan in advance of FY2014 to remove the deployment of one CG to the Middle East, two salvage ships to Africa and South America and five large surface combatants to the Western Pacific. Most concerning, however, we will have two thirds less surge capacity in FY2014. Our planned presence to meet the GFMAP in FY 2015 and beyond will also be at risk because maintenance cancelled in FY2014 may result in ships being unable to deploy in future years. At a minimum this lost maintenance will reduce the service life of these ships.

Because of the mechanics of sequestration, we cannot reprogram (move) funds from other accounts into operations and maintenance to make up for the sequestered amount. As a result, within operations and maintenance, we have to "go where the money is" and find savings in training, maintenance, civilian personnel, and shore facilities. The reductions in fleet training we are compelled to make will result in only one non-deployed CSG and one ARG trained and ready for surge operations – notionally without these reductions there would be three of each ready to deploy within about two weeks.

We will be compelled to cancel or defer planned FY 2014 fleet maintenance, including 34 of 55 surface ship maintenance periods totaling about $950 million – all in private shipyards – and 191 of about 700 aircraft depot maintenance actions. This missed maintenance will inevitably take time off the expected service life of our ships and aircraft, which in turn will make it harder to sustain even the smaller fleet we will have if the BCA caps remain in place for the long term. For example, a recent Center for Naval Analysis study estimated cancelling and not making up one maintenance period at the ten-year point in a DDG's life will shorten its overall service life by about five years.

We will be compelled to keep in place our freeze on hiring for most civilian positions. Ashore we will continue to conduct only safety-essential renovation and modernization of facilities, further increasing the large backlog in that area.

(2) Investment accounts will be particularly impacted by sequestration in FY 2014, and we will not be able to use prior-year funds to mitigate shortfalls as we did in FY 2013. Without Congressional action or mitigating circumstances, the reductions imposed by sequestration and the limitations of a CR will compel us to:

• Cancel planned FY 2014 procurement of an SSN, an LCS and an AFSB; also, delay an SSN planned for FY 2015 procurement. Each of these would further worsen the reduction in fleet size, described earlier in this statement, that the BCA would compel us to make over the long term.

• Delay the planned start of construction on the first SSBN(X) from FY 2021 to FY 2022. This would cause us to be unable to meet U.S. Strategic Command presence requirements when the Ohio-class SSBN retires.

• Cancel procurement of 11 tactical aircraft (4 EA-18G Growler, 1 F-35C Lightning II, 1 E-2D Advanced Hawkeye, 2 P-8A Poseidon, 3 MH-60 Seahawk) and about 400 weapons, exacerbating future BCA-driven reductions in our capabilities to project power despite A2/AD threats.

• Delay delivery of USS GERALD R. FORD (CVN-78) by two years, extending the period of 10 CVN in service, and lowering surge capacity.

• Delay the mid-life overhaul of USS GEORGE WASHINGTON (CVN 73) scheduled for FY 2016, disrupting today's "heel-to-toe" CVN overhaul schedule and reducing near-term CVN capacity.

In order to avoid or remedy some of the FY 2014 impacts described above, we need Congress to approve authorization and appropriations bills. This would enable Navy to transfer funds, pursue innovative acquisition approaches, start new projects, increase production quantities, and complete ships. This would:

• Keep SSBN(X) on schedule to sustain required SSBN capacity after the Ohio class begins to retire.

• Buy two Virginia class SSN in FY 2014 as planned and keep FY 2015 SSN procurement on schedule. These actions will help maintain our undersea dominance and ability to project power despite A2/AD threats.

• Protect CVN-73's mid-life overhaul and complete CVN-78 on time to sustain CVN capacity.

• Build the planned AFSB in FY 2014, which is needed to meet DSG and combatant commander presence requirements for CT/IW capability.

• Restore half of the cancelled surface ship maintenance availabilities to protect FY 2015 presence.[20]

September 1½ 2013, Navy ✳✳b✳✳ost

In a September 14, 2013, blog post, Rear Admiral John Kirby, the Navy's Chief of Information, stated:

> Lots of people are still talking about our ships in the eastern Mediterranean. And well they should.
>
> The President made it clear the other night that he still favors a strike, even as he pursues a diplomatic solution to the crisis in Syria.
>
> So, those destroyers are still out there. And they are still ready. As Secretary Mabus said just this week, "I guarantee you that if we are called upon to strike, we will strike hard and we will strike fast. Presence is what we do. It is who we are."
>
> But for all the attention we've received, two things keep getting lost in the clutter. First, those ships didn't surge to the Med. They were already there. We've been rotating two or three ballistic missile shooters through that region for several years now.
>
> And second, the forward presence they represent is no given. Well, maybe in the immediate future it is. But it's sure not going to be a given if sequestration remains the law of the land.

---

[20] Statement of Admiral Jonathan Greenert, U.S. Navy, Chief of Naval Operations, Before the House Armed Services Committee on Planning for Sequestration in FY 2014 and Perspectives of the Military Services on the Strategic Choices and Management Review, September 18, 2013, pp. 11-13.

Now, some folks might say we're exaggerating about that—that we're using the Syria situation as a way to plug a better budget.

Well, consider this. If sequestration hits us square in the face again next year—and I see nothing in the cards that says it won't—we'll be able to keep one carrier strike group and one amphibious ready group deployed to both the Pacific and the Central Command regions. And we'll be able to keep another of each ready to go if needed. But not a whole heckuva lot more than that.

And those destroyers? Yea, we'll still keep them over there in the eastern Med. It's an important mission. But the only way we will maintain that presence is by basing destroyers in Spain, which we will do starting next year.

In fact, if sequestration continues into the next fiscal year, a lot of things are going to get real hard.

Another round of sequestration will cut the Navy's budget by 10 percent below our FY14 budget submission. Worse, it will again apply the arbitrary, across-the-board cuts to our accounts. And since the President exempted military manpower from the cuts, sequestration essentially whacks a whopping 14 percent from every other account.

But this time, we won't have prior-year funds to ease the sting. We won't have that flexibility because resources from previous years' budgets have already been spent. There's no piggy bank to crack open.

Well, what about reprogramming authority? Wouldn't that help? Sure it would. We'd love to be able to move some money around. But even with reprogramming authority under an FY14 Appropriations Bill—which, by the way, we don't have yet—sequestration would cut our operations and maintenance account by $4.6 billion instead of $5.6 billion. That's the account we use to keep those ships out there and those Sailors fully trained.

A cut of this size to that account—without reprogramming authority—will delay more than half our ship maintenance availabilities next year and reduce our training to "just in time," meaning our Sailors won't be ready until just before they leave.

In fact, we'll have to shut down two airwings for three months each and limit four others to only the minimum level of flying, the "tactical hard deck."

Not only will we have fewer ships, subs and aircraft ready to go if needed, we'll also lose $4.5 billion next fiscal year from the accounts we use to buy new ones.

Sequestration could cost us a littoral combat ship, an afloat forward staging base/mobile landing platform, and up to 25 aircraft (Prowler, JSF, Osprey and others) needed for our future fleet. It will also delay a Virginia-class submarine.

And if we start the fiscal year with a continuing resolution, we will also delay the refueling of USS George Washington and won't be authorized to finish building the Gerald R. Ford.

We'll be forced to award contracts later than planned. And we'll no doubt miss out on multi-year procurement savings. That means the ships and planes we do buy are going to cost us more and come off the production lines and shipyards a little slower. And that means a smaller fleet.

A few weeks ago, Defense Secretary Hagel explained the Strategic Choices Management Review (SCMR), and the actions that could partially offset some of the damage sequestration in FY14 promises.

"The bold management reforms, compensation changes, and force structure reductions identified by the Strategic Choices and Management Review," he said, "can help reduce the damage that would be caused by the persistence of sequestration in fiscal year 2014. But they won't come close to avoiding it altogether. If these abrupt cuts remain, we risk fielding a force that over the next few years is unprepared due to a lack of training, maintenance, and the latest equipment."

So, SCMR options—including an eight or nine carrier fleet—is not out of the realm of the possible.

Of course, this isn't just about the carriers. If the numbers of strike groups shrink, so would the number of surface combatants, amphibious ships and air wings.

Indeed, if sequestration continues through this decade, the Navy will have something like 38 fewer ships to meet Combatant Commanders' needs—needs which are unlikely to decrease.

And it won't just be the Combatant Commanders who suffer. Just this month, we let contracts in Grand Rapids, MI; Cedar Rapids, IA; Columbia City, IN; Rolling Meadows, IL, and North Charleston, SC, and a host of other cities and small towns across America.

A smaller fleet means fewer jobs and lost revenue for small businesses and an unstable industrial base.

Just look around. The Navy is in demand. Heavy demand. From the Asia-Pacific to the eastern Mediterranean, we really are, as the CNO likes to say, "where it matters, when it matters."

But with the prospect of another sequestered year ahead, I wonder just how long we'll be able to keep that up.[21]

September ✱ 2013, ✱N✱ ✱emar✱s

At a September 5, 2013, event at the American Enterprise Institute (AEI), Admiral Jonathan Greenert stated:

So as we look into [FY]14, we had about $11 billion reduction in [FY]'13. Well, it's $14 billion in [FY]'14. It's ten percent.

We again, as you probably have read, have exempted manpower [from the FY2014 sequester] and it's the right thing to do. That means instead of [a] ten percent [reduction] for [the remaining] appropriations, the [remaining] appropriations that receive a reduction, [the] non-manpower [appropriation,] gets a 14 percent reduction.

What's going to be the impact? Well, subject to any action and help from the Congress as we move ahead, we'll probably have to cancel about half of our surface ship [maintenance]

---

[21] John Kirby, "U.S. Navy Presence At Risk Under Sequester," Navy Live (http://navylive.dodlive mil), September 14, 2013, accessed September 24, 2013, at http://navylive.dodlive mil/2013/09/14/presence-at-risk-under-sequester/.

availabilit[ies], so that's 34 [canceled surface ship maintenance availabilities]. We'll cancel a lot of aircraft [maintenance] availabilities]. [That's] About 190 [aircraft maintenance availabilities]. Last year we canceled about 90. So we're getting a backlog that is concerning in that regard. It will take a long time.

If we restore the budget after [FY]'14 and say okay. I'll tell you what. You've got full up operations and maintenance budget, it will take about five years to get that backlog in aircraft maintenance down.

Navy-wide, we'll reduce training for those who are not going to deploy. That gets back to that surge element that I mentioned before, reduction in that regard. So those that are not deploying in FY14 will have less training.

We'll have some air wings that will go to what we call tactical hard deck, which means they'll fly, the pilots will fly and the air crews will receive training at a level which is really just above what we're comfortable with for safety of flight, and it gets them at a point where when they get ready to deploy they can ramp up relatively quickly.

There's nothing magic about it. It's a statistical point. Not where I want to be. I will be pursuing to see if we can get more flying money to train our pilots above that level and get our kids to sea more often in FY14 as we look for reprogramming opportunity, the ability to move money.

So again [i.e., as in FY2013,] our surge capacity, I predict, will be about one-third of the norm as we look into [FY]'14.

Remember, sequestration is, and we're assuming it occurs in FY14, it takes reduction in every single account. So our shipbuilding reductions, which we were able to attenuate with prior money in [FY]'13, will take a hit in [FY]'14. I would see a loss of ta [sic: a] littoral combat ship there, again without help; an afloat forward staging base [AFSB], which is an important part of our future; and advance procurement for our Virginia Class submarine; and for [aircraft] carrier [refueling complex] overhaul [RCOH].

We might lose two more [ships from the FY2014 shipbuilding account, namely], we might lose a submarine procurement in [FY]'14, and a destroyer, again, if we are unable to reprogram, to move money into those shipbuilding accounts from other accounts.

These will be challenges, these will be issues we'll be working with the Congress as we move ahead.

In aircraft [procurement] we'll probably lose about 25 aircraft. If you say what kind? We'll say there isn't any that won't probably be lost. Some helos, the P-8s, to F-35s, they'll all be affected by this because it goes to every single account.

[The] CIVPERS [civilian personnel] hiring freeze will probably continue through that period. There's a great potential we'll have to do a RIF, a reduction in force, in our civilian work force. So we'll start a voluntary program probably immediately in [FY]'14, offering programs for voluntary retirement to help attenuate the need to have to do a reduction in force.

The key to all of this is this transfer, being able to transfer money to get reprogramming for us, in order to have a balanced approach. If I were to estimate what I think we need, we need about a billion dollars to get into the operations and maintenance account, and about a billion dollars to get into the procurement account so we can get that into shipbuilding which will be our number one priority in the Navy.[22]

August 1, 2013, Navy Testimony

At an August 1, 2013, hearing before the Seapower and Projection Forces subcommittee and the Readiness subcommittee of the House Armed Services Committee on Navy surface ship maintenance and readiness, the Navy testified:

Future Readiness

The biggest challenge to future surface ship readiness during these fiscally constrained times is finding the correct balance between funding the necessary maintenance, to provide ready forces now, and executing life cycle maintenance that ensures the long term viability of our ships. As the Navy learned in the report of the 2010 Fleet Review Panel, the impact of delaying maintenance is significant, since the cost and duration of deferred repairs rise exponentially. The end result will be ships being decommissioned before their expected service life (ESL) due to degraded material condition.

Today, we are prioritizing current readiness over future readiness; however, this is not sustainable over the long-term. If we choose to neglect life cycle maintenance, the material condition of our ships will continue to degrade to the point that they may be unable to deploy or conduct routine operations, culminating in decommissioning ships before their ESL. Even when the trend is reversed and more funding is made available for future readiness (operations, training, and maintenance); it will take a significant amount of time to restore our readiness to levels that support both typical presence as well as surge requirements.

Future readiness will also be at risk if we fail to maintain the necessary capabilities and capacity in our ship repair industrial base. Variations in workload can cause peaks and valleys in the skilled labor demand of our industrial base. We cannot afford to lose the skilled labor force we need to maintain our highly complex ships.

Today, our maintenance and modernization process, to include government oversight of the private sector work, is extremely challenged by sequestration and furloughs. There have been disruptions to basic waterfront services. Inspection of critical check points is stressed. Testing is being delayed, as is the ability to place work on contract and modify it as circumstances warrant. Under the furloughs, our Regional Maintenance Centers are operating at approximately 64% manning for Contract Management and Oversight (CMO). Similar shortages are occurring in first responder technical assistance positions. As a result, it is estimated that availabilities will experience increases in duration of 20 or more days. Delays and impacts have been observed onboard USS ROSS, USS MILIUS, USS COMSTOCK, USS LABOON and USS MITSCHER.

We are concerned that the Navy's budget challenges will be greatly exacerbated in FY14 and beyond. FY14 sequestration will result in a $14B [billion] budget shortfall in the Navy, which will have a significant impact on our operations and maintenance accounts and will derail the efforts the Navy has made to restore the material condition of our surface fleet. Our

---

[22] Transcript of remarks by Admiral Jonathan Greenert, Chief of Naval Operations, at the American Enterprise Institute (AEI), September 5, 2013, on American Military Strategy In A Time of Declining Budgets, provided to CRS by Navy Office of Legislative Affairs, September 6, 2013.

current estimate is that approximately 64% of the FY14 surface ship availabilities will be at risk in the event of an FY14 sequester (absent reprogramming). These availabilities are necessary to repair broken equipment and upgrade obsolete systems needed for deployment, and to ensure each ship reaches its ESL of thirty-five to forty years.[23]

July 19, 2013, Navy Press Briefing

At a July 19, 2013, press briefing, Admiral Jonathan Greenert, the Chief of Naval Operations, stated that

> Turning quickly to '14, we're still working to understand the fiscal situation, if sequestration is the—really, the rule of the day, and looking at all of the programs and all of the appropriations. The simple math is, it'll cause each account to go down 10 percent. That's what sequestration is. It's an algorithm.
>
> For the Navy—for the Department of Defense, it's $52 billion. For the U.S. Navy, it's about $14 billion. Now, if manpower were excluded, as we did in '13, and we're still deliberating on that, all the accounts would go down 14 percent, because when you exclude one, it all goes to the other accounts.
>
> The difference in '13 and '14 is, in '13, in our investments accounts, when sequestration set in, where we had to do the reductions, we had what we call prior-year money. We had money available from previous appropriations and laws coming in that we used to get us through '13. That's not available in '14. And so the impact on the investments accounts will be deeper cuts and a concern.
>
> My goal, the secretary's goal would be to preserve shipbuilding and those ship contracts and those aviation contracts as much as possible, meet our forward presence requirements, as I mentioned before, and—because—and make sure we hold onto multiyear procurement. That is the most efficient way to purchase equipment and platforms. But, again, as we do that, that money—those reductions are real, and they'll take place in other accounts, as the case may be.
>
> In fiscal year '14, as we look at it now, I think there will be a significant reduction in our surface ship [maintenance] availabilities,[24] subject to a change. About half of the 60 availabilities that we have planned will have to be deferred. You can't buy those back right away. [A] Ship is available for a maintenance period. If you don't do that maintenance period and that ship is then called out to do other things, it's a missed opportunity. So it takes time to get back.
>
> Reduced certification training in FY '14 would affect FY '15 deployers, so we've got to reconcile that. We've got to watch our air wing readiness, folks coming back and shutting down due to inability to have money because they're not deploying right away. You can't get down far, deep into the readiness bathtub, as we would call it. It makes it that much harder to get out, so we'll have to watch that very closely. And, again, a reduced ship procurement

---

[23] Statement of Rear Admiral Thomas Rowden, Director, Surface Warfare (N96) and Rear Admiral Timothy Matthews, Director, Fleet Readiness (N43) on Ensuring Navy Surface Force Effectiveness With limited Maintenance Resources before the House Armed Services Committee Subcommittee on Seapower and Projection Forces and Subcommittee on Readiness, August 1, 2013, pp. 2-3.

[24] A maintenance availability is a Navy term for a maintenance action, such as an overhaul.

would—and a break in a multiyear would cause each follow-on year's procurement of those ships that much more costly. So it's a very inefficient way to approach it.

The results for presence and for both '14 and '15, to kind of summarize, one carrier strike group, one amphibious ready group, each in each theater, Western Pacific and the Arabian Gulf. Our surge will be limited, really, to those that are next to deploy. They'll be ready to deploy with all the capabilities. But the rest of the fleet, regrettably, won't have the capabilities that we would notionally have and that we like to have in our plans to support.

The bottom line for all of this, I would ask you to think about, is the importance of being able to reprogram and being able to balance our accounts. Everything I kind of pass to you is all about an algorithm, a reduction across each account, and we need the ability, if you will, to be able to balance that.

Let me shift to people real quickly and then we'll go to questions and answers. As I mentioned before, they're the foundation of what we're about and what makes your Navy the finest Navy in the world. But we also have civilian shipmates, and regrettably, we're in the— we're enduring furloughs, and it's an impact. I felt it last week; I feel it this week. Just here at the staff, we feel it all around the Navy here or there.

Civilians are an integral part of our team. And we're committed to finding offsets to limit those effects whenever possible. We're looking at solutions, but it's got to be a Department of Defense-wide solution as we approach this.

We realize there's a financial burden. And it's regrettable. And it hurts our readiness, and it hurts our productivity, as well. And if sequestration continues into '14, we're going to need very closely—look very closely at that, at furloughs and, in my view, attempt to avoid it as much as feasible.[25]

During the subsequent question-and-answer portion of the briefing, the following exchange occurred:

Q: ... hello, sir. Two sequester-related questions, our favorite topic. One is, you were talking about capabilities we are missing, if we need to, you know, surge ships. Capabilities is a little vague. I presume it means more than, oh, gee, they're not sticker stocked in the onboard vending machines. It's probably a little bit more complicated and serious than that.

And, two, with this reprogramming you have pending, the Air Force got a bunch of grounded squadrons back in the air. Are you guys hoping, planning to have any similar reversals of bad fortune and get things back? You mentioned the ship's maintenance availabilities. And what capabilities have we lost? What can we get back?

ADM. GREENERT: When I speak to capabilities, Sydney, as an example, if you take an air wing, they do air-to-air, they do air-to-ground, they do a whole series of missions that the pilots are qualified to do, typically measured in how many cockpit hours you have in the air, how much you fly.

And so what will happen is, when you are unable to fully fund it and you're called upon, you have to reconcile, what missions will these pilots, in the case of an air wing, be qualified to do and certified to, so that we can report to the theater, hey, you're going to get an all up

---

[25] Department of Defense Press Briefing by Adm. Greenert in the Pentagon Briefing Room, July 19, 2013, accessed August 7, 2013, at http://www.defense.gov/transcripts/transcript.aspx?transcriptid=5278.

round in this particular mission in this regard. Similarly, with a destroyer or with a cruiser, what are they certified to do?

So we would have to tailor more, something we don't like to do, because the world is dynamic and they get a pretty big vote in what kind of operations we have, so we will typically certify our people for a range of operations and missions and certifications.

Q: So it's a matter of being trained to—to standard on the full range of things that you want people to do?

ADM. GREENERT: That's correct, because as you know—and in the past, we've had that—a carrier strike group or any of our units can swing theater to theater. Very different—well, somewhat different series of operations in, say, the Arabian Gulf, the North Arabian Sea versus the Western Pacific versus the Eastern Mediterranean.

STAFF: Dan?

Q: If you could just kind of relate what you said about piracy to sequestration and resources and so on, how—does that mean that you're not—the U.S. Navy will not be able to respond to that piracy problem as it might have two years ago or a year ago because of sequestration? And a related question. Could you go over again how U.S. naval capabilities are being affected and will be affected in the gulf, given this—these budget cuts that are coming?

ADM. GREENERT: The—the piracy question, the mission of counter- piracy is—the skill sets involved in that are more inherent in what we do as a Navy who is used to expeditionary operations around the world. So I would tell you, that—excuse me—that is a skill set that we can quickly revive and that doesn't concern me as much. In other words, those folks that are in theater, even if called on short notice, I think—I'm pretty comfortable in their counter-piracy capability.

Now, there is a skill set that is called visit, board, search and seizure. And that's basically coming—pulling alongside, either through a small boat or dropping through a helicopter, and that's kind of getting high end in that regard. That's a little different. That takes some practice. But typical, counter-piracy reporting, maybe bringing in a law enforcement detachment, we can do that relatively short order.

Your second question, capabilities affected in the Arabian Gulf as we move ahead. Again, it would depend on the mission, and it would depend on the requirements of the Central Command. The broad range of missions that we take there, ballistic missile defense, maritime intercept, sea control, as you mentioned, counter-piracy, all the way up to surface-to-surface missiles, you know, launching, counter- mining, that broad view we have to look at and perhaps tailor by—by unit, because the units—because of the money that we receive being so hard to predict out ahead. It would be a little different for each unit, so we have to watch this very closely on who we would send, if called upon in a contingency.

But let me enforce that those that we send over now, those that we'll send over in '14, they will be trained for the full range of missions. I'm right now talking about those that would surge if called upon in a broader contingency. Did I answer your question yet?

Q: Yeah, and then just could you—again, how do you see the carrier group presence evolving over the next year or two, given—with sequestration?

ADM. GREENERT: It will be one in the Western Pacific carrier strike group, one in the Arabian Gulf for—you know, 1-0 [1.0], as we call, it one-one in each theater.

Q: And that's sustainable, even with sequestration?

ADM. GREENERT: For—through '14, as we currently are aligned in our budget. When I get into the '14 budget and I get into the details, may have to alter that, but that's—that's what I see right now in my planning.

Q: Just a follow-up on that, does that mean that this on carrier strike group presence in the gulf in FY '14 is—does that mean that the Navy relinquishes its goal of 1.7 ratio in the region?

ADM. GREENERT: Well, the relinquishing would be, I guess, a good choice of words. What that—what we have to do is we came forward and said, "Here is our fiscal situation. Here is our forward presence situation aligned to that fiscal situation. We have to make a choice."

In a given year, we could send 1.7 over, but that money spent on operations this year would be invested there, not in training. It just wouldn't be enough. And therefore, you're mortgaging next year's—or you're foreclosing, I should say, next year's deployment, because those folks will not be trained, unless somehow you scramble and get money through the year, and that would be high risk.

So these are the—these are the discussions we had. We had these discussions early this year on the subject of the Truman deployment. And the simple choice was, we can continue the 1.7 and send the Harry Truman or—but that would be problematic for next year's deployment—or we could hold that, and it was determined overall that the right decision was—and it's a deliberate process, Matthew. It's the global force management process, approved by the secretary of defense.[26]

Later in the question-and-answer portion of the briefing, the following exchange occurred:

Q: Admiral. I wanted to ask on sequestration (inaudible) and you have no prior (inaudible) you have lots of ships under contract. Are you considering canceling contracts? Or how will you take (inaudible) cancel contracts?

ADM. GREENERT: It's a good question. What we need to do and what we're doing is, you sit down and you look at the contract, and what have you contracted—specifically have you contracted to do? What's in each line item? And how much does that cost? Is it feasible, for example, to—when you build a ship, for example, you get the ship, you get documentation, you get some ancillary gear, and you get some support, and you actually get some outfitting spares to get you through the first number of years until industry, who you contract for can procure the spares into the future.

So you say, all right, can we continue—can we keep this under contract at what might be 14 percent less than we had originally in the budget and then deal with as you're building the ship, deal with it maybe later? Is that feasible? And we will do that with each of the builders. That's a notional example. It's not precise, but it's notional.

These are the things that we'll have to do. Some of the things we buy have that sort of flex into them, and some of them don't. And if they don't, we'll lose the unit. And if you lose the unit, all the other ones in the contract, that price will go up accordingly.

---

[26] Department of Defense Press Briefing by Adm. Greenert in the Pentagon Briefing Room, July 19, 2013, accessed August 7, 2013, at http://www.defense.gov/transcripts/transcript.aspx?transcriptid=5278.

Q: Do you think, if you have sequestration in 2014, the goal of having 300 ships by the end of the decade, is that pretty much the goal?

ADM. GREENERT: I would be hard-pressed to say it is out. If we can retain the ships under contract in that multi-year that I mentioned before, where each one costs significantly less because you're buying them in bulk, if you will, or in larger quantities, if we can't, then those—those multi-years sort of unravel. The unit price goes up. You have less money, and this just starts spiraling down. If sequestration continues beyond '14, I'm pretty confident that it would be—we would not be able to meet those goals. That's too much at $50 billion a year.[27]

✽ ay 8, 2013, Navy Testimony

At a May 8, 2013, hearing on Navy shipbuilding programs before the Seapower subcommittee of the Senate Armed Services Committee, Sean Stackley, the Assistant Secretary of the Navy for Research, Development and Acquisition (i.e., the Navy's acquisition executive), stated the following in response to a question about the potential impact of a sequester on FY2014 funding:

Let me first say that Secretary [of Defense Chuck] Hagel has, in fact, chartered a Strategic Choices and Management Review to go directly at that question.

The Armed Services Committee has sent out a letter to the secretary asking for a more discrete response to the potentially $52 billion [DOD-wide] impact [of sequestration] in 2014, and that response is being addressed in the real-time.

Now, let me just talk about shipbuilding and make some assumptions. If the $52 billion impact [equates to] about 10 percent [of the DOD budget] and if that was prorated across all her lines than in shipbuilding [sic: all the line items in shipbuilding?], we will be looking at greater than $1 billion reduction to the 2014 [shipbuilding] request. That's assuming no ability to prioritize our investments. That will be applying sequestration in '14 just like it was in '13 line by line.

In 2013, shipbuilding took about a $1.7 billion reduction. We're able to manage that to a great extent to the prior year [sic]. We had assets that we are building in the prior year, so we were able to pay off about a third to 40 percent of sequestration by liquidating those assets.

Of the balance, $1 billion to $1.2 billion, some of that we are able to reduce our requirements. Some of that we're going to have to work within '13 and some of it effectively (inaudible) [sic: we have to shift?] into the outyears.

If you then do that again in 2014, effectively we have pulled all the margin out of the system in shipbuilding. Where we had margin, we have pulled it out. So now if we double-down sequestration in 2014, the margin is gone and now we're looking at direct impacts to the— our ship procurement rates.[28]

---

[27] Department of Defense Press Briefing by Adm. Greenert in the Pentagon Briefing Room, July 19, 2013, accessed August 7, 2013, at http://www.defense.gov/transcripts/transcript.aspx?transcriptid=5278.

[28] Transcript of hearing.

☀otentia☀☀mpa☀t on Si☀e o☀Navy o☀☀e☀☀in☀☀☀☀ Spen☀in☀to ☀o☀er ☀☀☀ ☀aps T☀ro☀☀☀ ☀☀2021

Another potential issue for Congress concerns the potential impact on the size of the Navy of reducing DOD spending (through sequestration or regular appropriations activity) in FY2013-FY2021 to levels at or near the lower caps established in the Budget Control Act of 2011, or BCA (S. 365/P.L. 112-25 of August 2, 2011). Navy officials state that a decision to reduce DOD's budget to such levels would eventually lead to a smaller Navy.

November ☀ 2013, Navy Testimony

At a November, 7, 2013, hearing before the Senate Armed Services Committee on the impact of sequestration on the national defense, Admiral Jonathan Greenert testified, in a statement similar to the one he used at the September 18, 2013, hearing discussed below, that

> Consistent with what the Deputy Secretary of Defense told this committee in August, if fiscally constrained to the revised discretionary caps, over the long term (2013-2023), the Navy of 2020 would not be able to execute the missions described in the DSG. There are numerous ways to adjust Navy's portfolio of programs to meet the BCA revised discretionary caps. These are currently under deliberation within the department. As requested, the following provides perspective on the level and type of adjustments that will need to be made.
>
> Any scenario to address the fiscal constraints under current law must include sufficient readiness, capability and manpower to complement the force structure capacity of ships and aircraft. This balance would need to be maintained to ensure each unit will be effective, even if the overall fleet is not able to execute the DSG. There are, however, many ways to balance between force structure, readiness, capability and manpower.
>
> One potential fiscal and programmatic scenario would result in a "2020 Fleet" of about 255-260 ships, about 30 less than today, and about 40 less than Navy's PB-14 submission. It would include 1-2 fewer CSG, and 1-2 fewer ARG than today. This 2020 fleet would not meet the DSG requirements for the mission to Provide a Stabilizing Presence. As a result, Navy would be less able to reinforce deterrence, build alliances and partnerships and influence events abroad.
>
> • Navy would not increase our global deployed presence, which would remain at about 95 ships in 2020. The lethality inherent in this presence, based on ship type deployed, would be less than today's 95-ship presence.
>
> • Navy would not increase presence in the Asia-Pacific, which would stay at about 50 ships in 2020. This would largely negate the ship force structure portion of our plan to rebalance to the Asia Pacific region directed by the DSG.
>
> • Navy would not "place a premium on U.S. military presence in—and in support of—partner nations" in the Middle East, since presence would decrease and, assuming we use the same ship deployment scheme in the future, there would be gaps in CSG presence totaling 2-3 months each year.
>
> • Navy would still "evolve our posture" in Europe by meeting our ballistic missile defense European Phased Adaptive Approach (EPAA) requirements with four BMD-capable DDG homeported in Rota, Spain and two land based sites in Romania and Poland. Additional

presence would still be provided by forward operating JHSV, MLP, AFSB and some rotationally deployed combatants.

• Navy would still provide "innovative, low-cost, and small-footprint approaches" to security in Africa and South America by deploying, on average, one JHSV and one LCS continuously to both regions and maintaining an AFSB in AFRICOM's area of responsibility.

In order to sustain a balance of force structure (current and future), modernization and personnel within our portfolio, continued compliance with the BCA revised discretionary caps would compel us to reduce our investments in force structure and modernization, which would result in a "2020 Fleet" that would not meet DSG direction in the following mission areas:

Counter Terrorism and Irregular Warfare (CT/IW). We would not have the capacity to conduct widely distributed CT/IW missions, as defined in the DSG. There would be inadequate LCS available to allocate to this non-core Navy mission, in the amount defined by the FSA and concurred upon by Special Operations Command.

Deter and Defeat Aggression. We would not be able to conduct one large-scale operation and also counter aggression by an opportunistic aggressor in a second theater. In this scenario, the fleet would have 9-10 CVN/CSG and 9-10 LHA/D and ARG. We would be able to sustain about one non-deployed CSG and one non-deployed ARG fully certified and able to surge on required timelines. Together, our presence and surge forces would be sufficient to conduct all missions associated with only one large scale operation, as defined today. This overall force and associated readiness would, however, be sufficient to execute Navy elements of the DSG mission to Conduct Stability and Counterinsurgency Operations.

Project Power Despite Anti-Access/Area Denial (A2/AD) Challenges. Overall, in this scenario, development of our capabilities to project power would not stay ahead of potential adversaries' A2/AD capabilities. We will not meet the projected capability requirements to assure Joint access in a plausible operational scenario in 2020 due to shortfalls, in particular, in air and missile defense:

• Some undersea capabilities will be slowed:

• Attainment of the required P-8A inventory (117) would be delayed from 2019 to 2020, and transition from the P-3C to the P-8A would be delayed from 2019 to 2020.

• Anti-submarine warfare combat system upgrades for DDGs and MFTA installations would not be affected.

• The LCS ASW Mission Package would be delayed from 2016 to 2017.

• Upgraded sonobuoys and advanced torpedo procurement would still equip all of our helicopters, SSN, and P-8A in the Western Pacific by 2018.

• Virginia Payload Module (VPM) would still be fielded in 2027 to enable Virginia-class SSN to replace SSGN that begin retiring in 2026.

• The LCS mine warfare mission package would still field its first increment in 2015 and the second in 2019.

• Air and missile defense improvements would be slowed:

• SEWIP upgraded electromagnetic sensing and upgraded jamming and deception capabilities would both be delayed one year (to 2015 and 2018, respectively). Both of these upgrades are required to counter advances in adversary anti-ship cruise missiles.

• The new Air and Missile Defense Radar (AMDR) would be delivered on only four ships, as compared to seven under our PB-14 submission, between 2021 and 2024.

• The Evolved Sea Sparrow Missile (ESSM) Block II would still be fielded in 2020, with 80 missiles being delivered to deployed ships.

• The F-35C Lightning II, the carrier-based variant of the Joint Strike Fighter, would still field in 2019 and join our CVW forward homeported in the Western Pacific in 2020. Overall, the number of F-35 procured would decrease by about 30 aircraft in 2020.

• All components of the improved air-to-air IR "kill chain" that circumvents adversary radar jamming would be delayed by two years. The Infrared Search and Track (IRST) sensor system would field in 2018 and the improved longer-range IRST would not deliver until 2021. The new longer-range AIM-9X Block III missile would not be fielded until 2023.

• Improvements to the air-to-air RF "kill chain" would be slowed down as F/A-18E/F Block II Super Hornet anti-jamming upgrades would be delayed to 2020. The longer-range AIM-120D missile would still field in 2014 but equipping of all Pacific carrier air wings would be delayed by two years to 2022.

• The Navy Integrated Fire Control – Counter Air (NIFC-CA) network would still initially field with the E-2D Advanced Hawkeye in 2015, but only four CVW (compared to six in our PB-14 submission) would have it by 2020. Transition to the E-2D would be delayed three years to 2025.

Operate Effectively in Space and Cyber Space. Plans to recruit, hire and train 976 additional cyber operators and form 40 computer operations teams by 2017 would not be impacted. This is a priority in any fiscal scenario. However, the BCA's reduced funding levels would delay replacement of our cyber systems and decrease our ability to defend our networks.

Maintain a Safe, Secure, and Effective Nuclear Deterrent. We would still be able to sustain today's ballistic missile submarine (SSBN) force. The SSBN(X) would still deliver in 2030 to replace retiring Ohio class SSBN while meeting requirements for SSBN presence and surge. This is the top priority program for the Navy.

Defend the Homeland and Provide Support to Civil Authorities. We would still meet the capacity requirements for these missions.

Counter Weapons of Mass Destruction. We would still meet the presence requirements for this mission.

Conduct Humanitarian, Disaster Relief, and Other Operations. We would still meet the presence requirements for this mission.

The extent of the fiscal changes in the BCA, when compared to current program and budget levels, would compel Navy to request relief from several program mandates and force structure capacity limits, in order to sustain and build a fleet with a balance of ship types. For example, mandated limits govern the size of the force, minimum funding for certain activities and facilities, and changes to the number of personnel at a base.[29]

September 18, 2013, Navy Testimony

At a September 18, 2013, hearing before the House Armed Services Committee on planning for sequestration in FY2014 and perspectives of the military services on the Strategic Choices and Management Review (SCMR), Admiral Jonathan Greenert testified, in a statement similar to the one he used at the November 7, 2013, hearing discussed above, that

> Consistent with what the Deputy Secretary of Defense told this committee last month, if fiscally constrained to the revised discretionary caps, over the long term (2013-2023), the Navy of 2020 would not be able to execute the missions described in the DSG. There are numerous means and alternatives to adjust Navy's portfolio of programs. These are currently under deliberation within the department. As requested, the following provides perspective on the level and type of adjustments that will need to be made.

> Any scenario to address the fiscal constraints under current law must include sufficient readiness, capability and manpower to complement the force structure capacity of ships and aircraft. This balance would need to be maintained to ensure each unit will be effective, even if the overall fleet is not able to execute the DSG. There are, however, many ways to balance between force structure, readiness, capability and manpower. One potential fiscal and programmatic scenario would result in a "2020 Fleet" of about 255-260 ships, about 30 less than today, and about 40 less than Navy's PB-14 submission. It would include 1-2 fewer CSG, and 1-2 fewer ARG than today. With regard to the DSG and presence, in this particular scenario the "2020 Fleet":

> • Would not increase our global deployed presence, which would remain at about 95 ships in 2020. The lethality inherent in this presence, based on ship type deployed, would be less than today's 95-ship presence.

> • Would not increase presence in the Asia-Pacific, which would stay at about 50 ships in 2020. This would largely negate the ship force structure portion of our plan to rebalance to the Asia Pacific region directed by the DSG.

> • Would not "place a premium on U.S. military presence in—and in support of—partner nations" in the Middle East, since presence would decrease and, assuming we use the same ship deployment scheme in the future, there would be gaps in CSG presence totaling 2-3 months each year.

> • Would still "evolve our posture" in Europe by meeting our ballistic missile defense European Phased Adaptive Approach (EPAA) requirements with four BMD-capable DDG homeported in Rota, Spain and two land based sites in Romania and Poland. Additional presence would still be provided by forward operating JHSV, MLP, AFSB and some rotationally deployed combatants.

> • Would still provide "innovative, low-cost, and small-footprint approaches" to security in Africa and South America by deploying, on average, one JHSV and one LCS continuously to both regions and maintaining an AFSB in AFRICOM's area of responsibility.

---

[29] Statement of Admiral Jonathan Greenert, U.S. Navy, Chief of Naval Operations, Before the Senate Armed Services Committee on the Impact of Sequestration on the National Defense, November 7, 2013, pp. 7-11.

In order to sustain a balance of force structure (current and future), modernization and personnel within our portfolio, continued compliance with the current law discretionary caps would compel us to reduce our investments (force structure and modernization), which would result in a "2020 Fleet" that would not meet DSG direction in the following mission areas:

Counter Terrorism and Irregular Warfare (CT/IW). We would not have the capacity to conduct widely distributed CT/IW missions, as defined in the DSG. There would be inadequate LCS available to allocate to this non-core Navy mission, in the amount defined by the FSA and concurred to by Special Operations Command.

Deter and Defeat Aggression. We would not be able to conduct one large-scale operation and also counter aggression by an opportunistic aggressor in a second theater. In this scenario, the fleet would have 9-10 CVN/CSG and 9-10 LHA/D and ARG. We would be able to sustain about one non-deployed CSG and one non-deployed ARG ready and able to surge on required timelines to meet all missions associated with one large scale operation, as defined today.

Project Power Despite Anti-Access/Area Denial (A2/AD) Challenges. Overall, in this scenario, development of our capabilities to project power would not stay ahead of potential adversaries' A2/AD capabilities:

• Some undersea capabilities will be slowed:

    o Attainment of the required P-8A inventory (117) would be delayed from 2019 to 2020, and transition from the P-3C to the P-8A would be delayed from 2019 to 2020.

    o Anti-submarine warfare combat system upgrades for DDGs and MFTA installations would not be affected.

    o The LCS ASW Mission Package would be delayed from 2016 to 2017.

    o Upgraded sonobuoys and advanced torpedo procurement would still equip all of our helicopters, SSN, and P-8A in the Western Pacific by 2018.

    o Virginia Payload Module (VPM) would still be fielded in 2027 to enable Virginia-class SSN to replace SSGN that begin retiring in 2026.

    o The LCS mine warfare mission package would still field its first increment in 2015 and the second in 2019.

• Air and missile defense improvements would be slowed:

    o SEWIP upgraded electromagnetic sensing and upgraded jamming and deception capabilities would both be delayed one year (to 2015 and 2018, respectively). Both of these upgrades are required to counter advances in adversary anti-ship cruise missiles.

    o The new Air and Missile Defense Radar (AMDR) would be delivered on only four ships, as compared to seven under our PB-14 submission, between 2021 and 2024.

    o The Evolved Sea Sparrow Missile (ESSM) Block II would still be fielded in 2020, with 80 missiles being delivered to deployed ships.

o The F-35C Lightning II, the carrier-based variant of the Joint Strike Fighter, would still field in 2019 and join our CVW forward homeported in the Western Pacific in 2020. Overall, the number of F-35 procured would decrease by about 30 aircraft in 2020.

o All components of the improved air-to-air IR "kill chain" that circumvents adversary radar jamming would be delayed by two years. The Infrared Search and Track (IRST) sensor system would field in 2018 and the improved longer-range IRST would not deliver until 2021. The new longer-range AIM-9X Block III missile would not be fielded until 2023.

o Improvements to the air-to-air RF "kill chain" would be slowed down as F/A-18E/F Block II Super Hornet anti-jamming upgrades would be delayed to 2020. The longer-range AIM-120D missile would still field in 2014 but equipping of all Pacific carrier air wings would be delayed by two years to 2022.

o The Navy Integrated Fire Control – Counter Air (NIFC-CA) network would still initially field with the E-2D Advanced Hawkeye in 2015, but only four CVW, compared to six in our PB-14 submission, will have it by 2020. Transition to the E-2D would be delayed three years to 2025.

Operate Effectively in Space and Cyber Space. Plans to recruit, hire and train 976 additional cyber operators and form 40 computer operations teams by 2017 would not be impacted. This is a priority in any fiscal scenario.

Maintain a Safe, Secure, and Effective Nuclear Deterrent. We would still be able to sustain today's ballistic missile submarine (SSBN) force. The SSBN(X) would still deliver in 2030 to replace retiring Ohio class SSBN while meeting requirements for SSBN presence and surge. This is the top priority program for the Navy.

Defend the Homeland and Provide Support to Civil Authorities. We would still meet the capacity requirements for these missions.

Conduct Humanitarian, Disaster Relief, and Other Operations. We would continue to be able to support some missions with 2 ARG and 9 JHSV present overseas.

The extent of the fiscal changes in the BCA, when compared to current program and budget levels, would compel Navy to request relief from several program mandates and force structure capacity limits, in order to sustain and build a fleet with a balance of ship types. For example, mandated limits govern the size of the force, minimum funding for certain activities and facilities, and changes to the number of personnel at a base.[30]

September ⚜ 2013, ⚜N⚜ ⚜emar⚜s

At a September 5, 2013, event at the American Enterprise Institute (AEI), Admiral Greenert stated:

If you look out beyond [FY]'14, if you look at [FY]'15 through say the rest of that ten year period that the Budget Control Act is expected, we're looking right now in the building, in the Pentagon, among the services, we're building an alternative look from FY15-[FY]23 to

---

[30] Statement of Admiral Jonathan Greenert, U.S. Navy, Chief of Naval Operations, Before the House Armed Services Committee on Planning for Sequestration in FY 2014 and Perspectives of the Military Services on the Strategic Choices and Management Review, September 18, 2013, pp. 6-10.

say okay, if this continues and we just, rather than doing this year by year we just look at, what would this mean? And the Strategic Choices Management Review [SCMR] was a snapshot of that. It took scenarios and said well, if we looked at it this way, this would be the impact. It helped provide the Secretary of Defense that understanding of what kind of scenarios might be out there.

So we don't have "the" scenario now, but we have scenarios that we kind of lay in there.

My approach to this, it's going to be to make sure we maintain a credible and modern sea-based strategic [nuclear] deterrent. That's my number one program, the SSBNX [Ohio replacement ballistic missile submarine program] and the current Ohio [class SSBN] program, along with the command and control features and along with the [service life] extension of the [SSBNs' D-5 submarine-launched ballistic] missile [SLBM].

Next, we need to maximize forward presence. Using the forward deployed naval force, that's the concept we have in Japan and the concept we've been offered in Rota[, Spain] to bring ships, bring the Sailors and the families over there. We get great leverage from that. But also to forward station ships [in other locations] also. So forward presence.

Three, we've got to have adequate readiness. The ships that are deployed have to be ready because it's all that much important with a smaller budget with a smaller Navy, that Navy which is out and about is absolutely ready.

We've got to make sure that our asymmetric capabilities continue to be developed. The undersea domain, electronic warfare in the electromagnetic spectrum, the electromagnetic rail gun, our laser technology which is coming along. As you probably know, we are deploying a laser gun this coming summer, if you will, in the summer of [FY]'14 I should say, to the Arabian Gulf and we're looking to bring along the electronic rail gun.

[Two other priorities are] Cyber and people. Remember, people are an asymmetric advantage, so we've got to do that right.

We will reduce force structure in this plan, but we have to do it while preserving the right capacity to at least do one MCO [Major Contingency Operation, i.e., a major regional conflict] as we look out into the future, and we will have to reduce procurement. There's no doubt about it. I've got to look at the industrial base and make sure that as much as possible we're doing this in a deliberate and planned Navy.

That's kind of the principles of this look ahead.

Let me give you a scenario. If you say okay, what might you look like? And a scenario could be, in the future, if you take 2020 and you say what was your plan? Some of you may have seen this and say well, the plan [without sequestration] was to get to 295 ships with 116 planned to be deployed. That's in the red here [indicating on a briefing slide]. You say [in the future] future, if we had to retire a number of ships [due to defense spending being reduced to lower levels], [there] might [instead] be a 250 ship Navy in 2020, and able to get about 96 ships deployed.

A couple of thoughts about this. This is really leveraging operating forward, as I like to—It's one of my tenets in there. It's using the forward deployed naval force. Forward stationing ships. It's bringing along ships like the littoral combat ship [LCS] to join high speed vessel [JHSV], the afloat forward staging base [AFSB], and putting them in key areas of the world where we can leverage their usage. You get sort of a picture like that.

> There is not a lot of surge [capacity] here. This is a Navy which, you can do the math, 96 [deployed ships] divided by [a total fleet of] 257 [ships]. You see how much is forward and out and about.
>
> The reduction of our manpower associated with such a future where we reduce forces is completely connected to our force structure. What I mean by that is, we man equipment. That's the principle in the Navy with regard to manpower where some of the other services, they equip their manning. It's all about where our people are. And we have it about right now. We're just about where I want to be on the number of people per unit. So it's about retiring units, if you will, if you want to get a lot of savings out there as opposed to reducing people.
>
> There's also a compensation entitlement reform and an overhead reduction which is part and parcel to a future look, and we are studying that closely.
>
> I'll close now and say look, preserving presence is the key. That's our mandate, to be where it matters and to be ready when it matters, and we'll continue that rebalance to the Asia Pacific. We'll be moving ships forward. That's kind of a key element as I look into the future. And we've got to remain ready forward so we can do the things, like I showed you in the little graphic today. [The goal is to] Be able to respond quickly to what the nation needs.
>
> But throughout it all, Sailors and our civilian work force, our civilian sailors, are going to be the asymmetric advantage, are going to assure that we keep a force which is whole and not hollow.[31]

August 1, 2013, Navy Testimony

At an August 1, 2013, hearing before the Seapower and Projection Forces subcommittee and the Readiness subcommittee of the House Armed Services Committee on Navy surface ship maintenance and readiness, Rear Admiral Thomas Rowden, the Director for Surface Warfare, testified that

> Keeping our equipment properly operating and training sailors takes money and time. When required funding is limited through sequestration or for other reasons, we are forced to make hard decisions about what gets fixed and what training is completed.
>
> Make no mistake. We will deploy ready ships. But our ability to respond to contingencies and surge additional ships to a crisis could be reduced.
>
> In the long term, if we do not maintain our ships, the Navy will be forced to decommission ships before their expected service life—or before they reach their expected service life. We estimate that if sequestration continues over the long term, by 2020 we will be reduced from 295 ships down to 257 ships. Over the same period, we do not anticipate the combatant commanders' demand for ready forces will decrease.[32]

---

[31] Transcript of remarks by Admiral Jonathan Greenert, Chief of Naval Operations, at the American Enterprise Institute (AEI), September 5, 2013, on American Military Strategy In A Time of Declining Budgets, provided to CRS by Navy Office of Legislative Affairs, September 6, 2013.

[32] Transcript of hearing.

Later in the hearing, he stated: "There is no doubt, I think, that given where we are proposing to go with sequestration that it will reduce the number of ships that we have in the Navy, and I think probably by 2020, we're looking at about 257 ships."[33] Still later in the hearing, he stated that

> it goes back to the—the deferral of maintenance and the bow-waving of maintenance into successive years. If we have to defer X number this year and that pushes into the following fiscal year and we have to defer Y, eventually we get to the point where the cost to maintain those ships goes to the point where it's just not—it's not cost-effective to maintain those ships and therefore you start to remove them out of service early.

> Based on what we've seen, there's a potential that we could go down to as many as 257. I haven't estimated it beyond that. I don't know whether Admiral Matthews[34] has anything beyond the 2020 timeframe. But looking at where we think we may have to go in the next seven years, we're looking at about—we think we're looking at about 257 ships by the time we get to 2020.[35]

July 31, 2013, DOD Press Briefing

At a July 31, 2013, press briefing on the Strategic Choices and Management Review (SCMR)—a DOD study of potential options for accommodating reductions in future defense funding levels—Secretary of Defense Chuck Hagel stated that "sequester-level cuts" to defense funding could, among other things, "reduce the number of carrier strike groups from 11 to 8 or 9.... "[36]

April 16, 2013, Navy Testimony

At an April 16, 2013, hearing before the House Armed Services Committee on the Department of the Navy's proposed FY2014 budget, Admiral Greenert, in answer to a question about the impact of sequestration on the Navy, stated:

> Mr. Chairman, as I—as I look at the numbers, and I think you're—you're talking, assuming a sequestration, $500 billion. First thing I do is, and most important, we provide forward presence. And it's—I can't provide—I cannot meet the—the current Global Force Management Allocation Plan with those numbers. So I don't know what number I would be at. It would be on the order 30 ships [less than today], you know, as I look at a balanced reduction in that regard, less than the number of ships that I have today.

> So, let's say 250 ships if I'm at 280 today.[37]

---

[33] Transcript of hearing.

[34] The other Navy witness at the hearing was Rear Admiral Timothy Matthews, the Director for Fleet Readiness.

[35] Transcript of hearing.

[36] Department of Defense Press Briefing by Secretary Hagel and Adm. Winnefeld from the Pentagon, July 31, 2013, accessed August 7, 2013, at http://www.defense.gov/transcripts/transcript.aspx?transcriptid=5280.

[37] Transcript of hearing.

February 12, 2013, Navy Testimony

At a February 12, 2013, hearing before the Senate Armed Services Committee on the impacts of sequestration and/or a full-year continuing resolution on the Department of Defense, the Navy testified that:

> In addition to sequestration for FY13, the BCA also required the lowering of the discretionary caps for FY14 through FY21. Beyond FY13, if the discretionary cap reductions are sustained for the full nine years, we would fundamentally change the Navy as currently organized, trained and equipped. As time allows, we will take a deliberate and comprehensive approach to this reduction, based on a reevaluation of the Defense Strategic Guidance. In doing so, I will endeavor to: (1) ensure our people are properly resourced; (2) protect sufficient current readiness and warfighting capability; (3) sustain some ability to operate forward by continuing to forward base forces in Japan, Spain, Singapore and Bahrain, and by using rotational crews; and (4) maintain appropriate research and development.

> As I indicated last year to the Senate Armed Services Committee (SASC), under a set of fiscal circumstances in sequestration, our Navy may be a fleet of around 230 ships. That would be a loss of more than 50 ships, including the loss of at least two carrier strike groups. We would be compelled to retire ships early and reduce procurement of new ships and aircraft. This would result in a requisite reduction in our end strength. Every program will be affected and as Secretary Panetta noted in his 2011 letter to Senators McCain and Graham, programs such as the F-35 Lightning II, next generation ballistic missile submarine and Littoral Combat Ship might be reduced or terminated.[38]

Appropriate Future Size and Structure of Navy in Light of Strategic and Budgetary Changes

Another potential oversight issue for Congress concerns the appropriate future size and structure of the Navy. Changes in strategic and budgetary circumstances have led to a broad debate over the future size and structure of the military, including the Navy. Changes in strategic circumstances include, among other things, the end of U.S. combat operations in Iraq, the winding down of U.S. combat operations in Afghanistan, and China's military (including naval)

---

[38] Statement of Admiral Jonathan Greenert, Chief of Naval Operations, before the Senate Armed Services Committee on the Impact of Sequestration, February 12, 2013, pp. 8-9. Although the Navy's written statement for the hearing is from Admiral Greenert, the Navy's testimony at the hearing was actually given by the Vice Chief of Naval Operations, Admiral Mark E. Ferguson III, who was substituting for Admiral Greenert at the hearing. The Navy presented similar testimony at a similar hearing before the House Armed Services Committee on February 13, 2013.

Similarly, on October 22, 2012, Admiral Mark Ferguson, the Vice Chief of Naval Operations, stated, "If you project out 10 years—remember that the budget control act talks about 10 years of [funding] reductions—now you start talking about a fleet reduced to about 230-235 ships." (As quoted in David Smalley, "Leaner Navy Looking at Future Technology, Fleet Size and Sequestration," *Navy News Service*, October 23, 2012, accessed October 25, 2012 at http://www navy mil/submit/display.asp?story_id=70311.) On January 8, 2013, Vice Admiral William Burke, the Deputy Chief of Naval Operations for Warfare Systems, stated, "As a result of sequestration, what I testified to last year was we'll have, if sequestration is fully implemented, we'll have a force of about 230 ships.... I'm not talking about what the aviation numbers are, but they'll go down by a similar amount—a similar amount being 20 percent." (As quoted in Dan Taylor, "Adm. Burke: Navy Needs To Fill $2 Billion Hole When OCO Goes Away," *Inside the Navy*, January 14, 2013. See also Michael Fabey, "U.S. Navy Prioritizes Ship Total Ownership Costs, Maintenance," *Aerospace Daily & Defense Report*, January 9, 2013: 3.)

modernization effort.[39] Changes in budgetary circumstances center on reductions in planned levels of defense spending resulting from the Budget Control Act of 2011, or BCA (S. 365/P.L. 112-25 of August 2, 2011).

On January 5, 2012, the Administration announced that, in light of the end of U.S. combat operations in Iraq, the winding down of such operations in Afghanistan, and developments in the Asia-Pacific region, U.S. defense strategy in coming years will include a stronger focus on the Asia-Pacific region.[40] Since the Asia-Pacific region is primarily a maritime and aerospace theater for the DOD, this shift in strategic focus is expected by many observers to result in a shift in the allocation of DOD resources toward the Navy and Air Force. DOD officials have indicated that efforts to support a stronger focus on the Asia-Pacific region will be protected if planned levels of DOD spending in future years are reduced as a result of the BCA or other legislative action.

The Navy's current goal for a fleet of 306 ships reflects a number of judgments and planning factors (some of which the Navy receives from the Office of the Secretary of Defense), including but not limited to the following:

- U.S. interests and the U.S. role in the world, and the U.S. military strategy for supporting those interests and that role;

- current and projected Navy missions in support of U.S. military strategy, including both wartime operations and day-to-day forward-deployed operations;

- current and projected capabilities of potential adversaries, including their anti-access/area-denial (A2/AD) capabilities;

- regional combatant commander (COCOM) requests for forward-deployed Navy forces;

- the individual and networked capabilities of current and future Navy ships and aircraft;

- basing arrangements for Navy ships, including numbers and locations of ships homeported in foreign countries;

- maintenance and deployment cycles for Navy ships; and

- fiscal constraints.

With regard to the fourth point above, Navy officials testified at least three times in 2012 that a Navy of more than 500 ships would be required to fully meet COCOM requests for forward-deployed Navy forces (see **Appendix A**). The difference between a fleet of more than 500 ships and the current goal for a fleet of 306 ships can be viewed as one measure of the operational risk associated with the goal of a fleet of 306 ships. A goal for a fleet of more than 500 ships might be viewed as a fiscally unconstrained goal.

---

[39] For more on the modernization of China's military (particularly naval) capabilities and its potential implications for required U.S. Navy capabilities, see CRS Report RL33153, *China Naval Modernization: Implications for U.S. Navy Capabilities—Background and Issues for Congress*, by Ronald O'Rourke.

[40] Department of Defense, *Sustaining U.S. Global Leadership: Priorities for 21ˢᵗ Century Defense*, January 2012, 8 pp. For more on this document, see CRS Report R42146, *In Brief: Assessing the January 2012 Defense Strategic Guidance (DSG)*, by Catherine Dale and Pat Towell. See also CRS Report R42448, *Pivot to the Pacific? The Obama Administration's "Rebalancing" Toward Asia*, coordinated by Mark E. Manyin.

Some study groups have made their own proposals for Navy ship force structure that reflect their own perspectives on the points listed above (particularly the first three and the final one) shows some of these proposals. For purposes of comparison, also shows the Navy's 306-ship goal of January 2013.

Table 7. Recent Study Group Proposals for Navy Ship Force Structure

Ship type	Navy's 306-ship goal of January 2013	Project on Defense Alternatives (PDA) (November 2012)	Heritage Foundation (April 2011)	Cato Institute (September 2010)[a]	Independent Panel Assessment of 2010 QDR (July 2010)	Sustainable Defense Task Force (June 2010)	Center for a New American Security (CNAS) (November 2008)	Center for Strategic and Budgetary Assessments (CSBA) (2008)[b]
Submarines								
SSBN	12	7	14[c]	6	14	7	14	12
SSGN	0	6-7	4	0	4	4	0	2
SSN	48	42	55	40	55	37	40	41
Aircraft carriers								
CVN	11	9	11	8	11	9	8	11
CVE	0	0	0	0	0	0	0	4
Surface combatants								
Cruiser	88	72-74	88	22	n/a	85	18	14
Destroyer				65	n/a		56	73
Frigate	0	2-7[i]	28[d]	14	n/a	0	0	9[e]
LCS	52	12[j]		4	n/a	25	48	55
SSC	0	i	0	0	n/a	0	40	0[f]
Amphibious and Maritime Prepositioning Force (Future) (MPF[F]) ships								
Amphibious ships	33	≥23	37	23	n/a	27	36	33
MPF(F) ships	0	n/a	0	0	n/a	n/a	0	3[g]
LSD station ships	0	0	0	0	0	0	0	7[h]
Other: Mine warfare (MIW) ships; Combat Logistics Force (CLF) ships (i.e., at-sea resupply ships), and support ships								
MIW	0	14[i]	14	11	0	0	0	0
CLF ships	29	n/a	33	21	n/a	36	40	31
Support ships	33	n/a	25	27	n/a			31
TOTAL battle force ships	306	230	309	241	346	230	300	326[j]

Source: Table prepared by CRS based on the following sources: **For Heritage Foundation:** *A Strong National Defense[:] The Armed Forces America Needs and What They Will Cost*, Heritage Foundation, April 5, 2011, pp. 25-26. **For Cato Institute:** Benjamin H. Friedman and Christopher Preble, *Budgetary Savings from Military Restraint*, Washington, Cato Institute, September 23, 2010 (Policy Analysis No. 667), pp. 6, 8-10, and additional information provided by Cato Institute to CRS by e-mail on September 22, 2010. **For Independent Panel Assessment:** Stephen J. Hadley and William J. Perry, co-chairmen, et al., *The QDR in Perspective: Meeting America's National Security Needs In the 21st Century, The Final Report of the Quadrennial Defense Review Independent Panel*, Washington, 2010, Figure 3-2 on pages 58-59. **For Sustainable Defense Task Force:** *Debt, Deficits, and*

Defense, A Way Forward[:] Report of the Sustainable Defense Task Force, June 11, 2010, pp. 19-20. **For CNAS**: Frank Hoffman, *From Preponderance to Partnership: American Maritime Power in the 21st Century*. Washington, Center for a New American Security, November 2008. p. 19 (Table 2). **For CSBA**: Robert O. Work, *The US Navy[:] Charting a Course for Tomorrow's Fleet*. Washington, Center for Strategic and Budgetary Assessments, 2008. p. 81 (Figure 5). **For PDA**: Carl Conetta, Reasonable Defense, Project on Defense Alternatives, November 14, 2012, 31 pp.

Notes: n/a is not addressed in the report. **SSBN** is nuclear-powered ballistic missile submarine; **SSGN** is nuclear-powered cruise missile and special operations forces submarine; **SSN** is nuclear-powered attack submarine; **CVN** is large nuclear-powered aircraft carrier; **CVE** is medium-sized aircraft carrier; **LCS** is Littoral Combat Ship; **SSC** (an acronym created by CRS for this table) is small surface combatant of 1,000+ tons displacement—a ship similar to late-1990s Streetfighter concept; **MPF(F)** is Maritime Prepositioning Force (Future) ship; **LSD** is LSD-41/49 class amphibious ship operating as a station ship for a formation like a Global Fleet Station (GFS); **MIW** is mine warfare ship; **CLF** is combat logistics force (i.e., resupply) ship.

a. Figures shown are for the year 2020; for subsequent years, reductions from these figures would be considered.

b. Figures shown are for the year 2028.

c. The report calls for a force of 280 SLBMs, which appears to equate to a force of 14 SSBNs, each with 20 SLBM tubes.

d. The report calls for a force of 28 small surface combatants, and appears to use the term small surface combatants the same way that the Navy does in the 30-year shipbuilding plan—as a way of collectively referring to frigates and LCSs. The small surface combatants (SSCs) called for in the November 2008 CNAS report are separate from and smaller than the LCS.

e. Maritime Security Frigates.

f. Plan includes 28 patrol craft (PCs) of a few hundred tons displacement each, as well as 29 boat detachments and seven riverine squadrons.

g. Plan shows three Mobile Landing Platform (MLP) ships that the Navy currently plans for the MPF(F) squadron, plus 16 existing current-generation maritime prepositioning force (MPF) ships and 17 existing prepositioning ships for Army and other service/agency equipment. Plan also shows 67 other DOD sealift ships.

h. T-LSDs, meaning LSDs operated by the Military Sealift Command (MSC) with a partly civilian crew.

i. The CSBA report shows a total of 488 units by including 162 additional force units that do not count toward the 306-ship goal under the battle force ships counting method that has been used since the early 1980s for public policy discussions of the size of the Navy. These 162 additional force units include 16 existing current-generation maritime prepositioning force (MPF) ships and 17 existing prepositioning ships for Army and other service/agency equipment, 67 other DOD sealift ships, 28 PCs, 29 boat detachments, and certain other small-scale units. The CSBA report proposes a new counting method for naval/maritime forces that includes units such as these in the total count.

j. The report "prescribes ending procurement of the LCS with the 12 already purchased. The *Reasonable Defense* model foresees a future cohort of 28 to 33 small surface combatants, including a mix of the 12 LCS that have already been procured, 14 Mine Counter Measure (MCM) ships already in the fleet, and small frigates or ocean-going corvettes. As the MCM ships age and leave the fleet, the LCS should assume their role. The would leave a post-MCM requirement for 16 to 21 additional small surface combatants. For this, the Navy needs a simpler, less expensive alternative to the LCS."

A potential key question for Congress concerns whether the U.S. Navy in coming years will be large enough to adequately counter improved Chinese maritime A2/AD forces while also adequately performing other missions of interest to U.S. policymakers around the world. Some observers are concerned that a combination of growing Chinese naval capabilities and budget-driven reductions in the size of the U.S. Navy could encourage Chinese military overconfidence and demoralize U.S. allies and partners in the Pacific, and thereby make it harder for the United

States to defend its interests in the region.[41] Potential oversight questions for Congress include the following:

- Under the Administration's plans, will the Navy in coming years be large enough to adequately counter improved Chinese maritime A2/AD forces while also adequately performing other missions of interest to U.S. policymakers around the world?

- What might be the political and security implications in the Asia-Pacific region of a combination of growing Chinese naval capabilities and budget-driven reductions in the size of the U.S. Navy?

- If the Navy is reduced in size and priority is given to maintaining Navy forces in the Pacific, what will be the impact on Navy force levels in other parts of the world, such as the Persian Gulf/Indian Ocean region or the Mediterranean Sea, and consequently on the Navy's ability to adequately perform its missions in those parts of the world?

- To what extent could the operational impacts of a reduction in Navy ship numbers be mitigated through increased use of forward homeporting, multiple crewing, and long-duration deployments with crew rotation (i.e., "Sea Swap")? How feasible are these options, and what would be their potential costs and benefits?[42]

- Particularly in a situation of constrained DOD resources, if enough funding is allocated to the Navy to permit the Navy in coming years to maintain a fleet of 306 ships including 11 aircraft carriers, how much would other DOD programs need to be reduced, and what would be the operational implications of those program reductions in terms of DOD's overall ability to counter improved Chinese military forces and perform other missions?[43]

Sufficiency of 30-Year Shipbuilding Plan for Achieving Navy's 306-Ship Goal

Another potential oversight issue for Congress concerns the sufficiency of the Navy's 30-year shipbuilding plan for achieving the Navy's goal for a 306-ship fleet. The Navy's 30-year shipbuilding plans in recent years have generally not included enough ships to fully support all elements of the Navy's 306-ship goal over the long run. The Navy has projected that the fleet would remain below 306 ships during most of the 30-year period, and experience shortfalls at various points in cruisers-destroyers, attack submarines, and amphibious ships. In light of these

---

[41] See, for example, Dan Blumenthal and Michael Mazza, "Asia Needs a Larger U.S. Defense Budget," *Wall Street Journal*, July 5, 2011; J. Randy Forbes, "Defence Cuts Imperil US Asia Role," *The Diplomat* (http://the-diplomat.com), October 26, 2011. See also Andrew Krepinevich, "Panetta's Challenge," *Washington Post*, July 15, 2011: 15; Dean Cheng, *Sea Power and the Chinese State: China's Maritime Ambitions*, Heritage Foundation Backgrounder No. 2576, July 11, 2011, p. 10.

[42] For further discussion of these options, see CRS Report RS21338, *Navy Ship Deployments: New Approaches—Background and Issues for Congress*, by Ronald O'Rourke.

[43] For further discussion, see CRS Report RL33153, *China Naval Modernization: Implications for U.S. Navy Capabilities—Background and Issues for Congress*, by Ronald O'Rourke.

---

projected shortfalls, policymakers may wish to consider various options, including but not limited to the following:

- increasing planned procurement quantities of destroyers, attack submarines, and amphibious ships;

- extending, if feasible, the service lives of older destroyers and amphibious ships, and (if feasible) refueling and extending the service lives of a small number of older attack submarines; and

- reducing the Navy's ship force structure goals for destroyers, attack submarines, and/or amphibious ships.

The first two options would require increased funding for procurement and for operation and support (O&S) costs, respectively, while the third option could reduce the Navy's ability to perform its missions.

Affordability of 30-Year Shipbuilding Plan

Another potential oversight issue for Congress concerns the prospective affordability of the Navy's 30-year shipbuilding plan. In assessing the prospective affordability of the 30-year plan, key factors that Congress may consider include estimated ship procurement costs and future shipbuilding funding levels.

Estimated Ship Procurement Costs

As mentioned earlier, the Navy's 30-year shipbuilding plan is based on certain assumptions, including assumptions about ship procurement costs. If one or more Navy ship designs turn out to be more expensive to build than the Navy estimates, then the projected funding levels shown in the 30-year shipbuilding plan will not be sufficient to procure all the ships shown in the plan. Ship designs that can be viewed as posing a risk of being more expensive to build than the Navy estimates include Gerald R. Ford (CVN-78) class aircraft carriers (a program currently experiencing cost growth), Ohio-replacement (SSBNX) class ballistic missile submarines, the Flight III version of the DDG-51 destroyer, the TAO(X) oiler, and the LX(R) amphibious ship.

In recent years, the Congressional Budget Office (CBO) has estimated that certain Navy ships would be more expensive to procure than the Navy estimates, and consequently that the Navy's 30-year shipbuilding plan would cost more to implement than the Navy has estimated. In its October 2013 report on the cost of the FY2014 30-year shipbuilding plan, the CBO estimates that the plan would cost an average of $19.3 billion per year in constant FY2013 dollars to implement, or about 15% more than the Navy estimates. CBO's estimate is about 6% higher than the Navy's estimate for the first 10 years of the plan, about 14% higher than the Navy's estimate for the second 10 years of the plan, and about 26% higher than the Navy's estimate for the final 10 years of the plan.[44] Some of the difference between CBO's estimate and the Navy's estimate, particularly in the latter years of the plan, is due to a difference between CBO and the Navy in

---

[44] Congressional Budget Office, *An Analysis of the Navy's Fiscal Year 2014 Shipbuilding Plan*, October 2013, Table 3 (page 13).

how to treat inflation in Navy shipbuilding. **Table 8** summarizes the Navy and CBO estimates of the FY2014 30-year shipbuilding plans.

Table 8. Navy and CBO Estimates of Cost of FY2014 30-Year (FY2014-FY2043) Shipbuilding Plans

Funding for new-construction ships, in billions of constant FY2013 dollars

	First 10 years (FY2014-FY2023)	Next 10 years (FY2024-FY2033)	Final 10 years (FY2034-FY2043)	Entire 30 years (FY2014-FY2043)
Navy estimate	15.4	19.8	15.2	16.8
CBO estimate	16.3	22.6	19.1	19.3
% difference between Navy and CBO estimates	6%	14%	26%	15%

Source: Congressional Budget Office, *An Analysis of the Navy's Fiscal Year 2014 Shipbuilding Plan*, October 2013, Table 3 (page 13).

Future Shipbuilding Funding Levels

As mentioned earlier, the Navy's 30-year shipbuilding plan is based on certain assumptions, including assumptions about future shipbuilding funding levels. It has been known for some time that funding requirements for the Ohio-replacement (SSBN[X]) ballistic missile submarine program will put considerable pressure on the shipbuilding budget during the middle years of the 30-year plan. Although the FY2014 30-year shipbuilding plan reduces procurement of other types of ships in the middle years of the plan to help accommodate the SSBN(X) program, the Navy still projects that the shipbuilding budget would need to be substantially higher during the middle years of the plan than during the earlier or later years of the plan.

If the "hump" in shipbuilding funding during the middle years of the 30-year plan is not achieved, numerous ships shown for procurement during the middle years of the plan might not be procured. A potential oversight question for Congress is whether the Navy has received a commitment or assurance of some kind from DOD leaders that the Navy will be able to budget for the "hump" in shipbuilding funding during the middle years of the 30-year plan without reducing funding for other Navy program priorities. The Navy's report on the FY2014 30-year shipbuilding plan states:

> The Department [of the Navy] will encounter several challenges in executing this shipbuilding plan; perhaps the most important is funding and delivering the *Ohio*-replacement (OR) program SSBN. The OR SSBN is projected to cost about $6 billion each [in constant FY2013 dollars]. Therefore, during the procurement and construction of OR SSBN between FY2021 and FY2035 an average of $19.2 billion per year is projected to be required for shipbuilding, which will be a key resourcing challenge for the Department.
>
> In addition to the challenge of funding the OR SSBN, during several years in the early 20202 [the] Navy will also require approximately $2 billion [per year] in additional ship construction funding to recapitalize the large number of ships decommissioning in those years. Our current fleet has a large cohort of ships that are about the same age and will thus retire as a group. These ships were built in the 1980s, some at a rate of three or four ships per year per class. These retiring ships will need to be recapitalized to reach the FSA-required battle force size and shape [i.e., the 306-ship goal]....

DoN has historically been able to resource between $12B [billion] and $14B in annual new-ship procurement funding. During the FY2014-FY2018 FYDP, average annual new-ship procurement funding is about $14B. This level of investment is based on the need to balance our resources between manning, maintenance, sustainment, modernization and recapitalization of our ships, aircraft and weapons.

The cost of the OR SSBN is significant relative to the resources available to DoN in any given year. At the same time, the Department will have to address the block retirement of ships procured in large numbers during the 1980s which are reaching the end of their service lives. The confluence of these events prevents DoN from being able to shift resources within the shipbuilding account to accommodate the cost of the OR SSBN.

If DoN funds the OR SSBN from within its own resources, OR SSBN construction will take away from construction of other ships in the battle force such as attack submarines, destroyers, aircraft carriers and amphibious warfare shps. The resulting battle force will not meet the requirements of the FSA and will therefore not be sufficient to implement the DSG [Defense Strategic Guidance]. In addition there will be significant impact to the shipbuilding industrial base.[45]

A May 2, 2013, press report states:

[Vice Admiral William Burke, Deputy Chief of Naval Operations for Warfare Systems], who is set to retire in the next few weeks,[46] spoke frankly about the undersea portion of the U.S. strategic nuclear triad "and its intersection with our shipbuilding plan."

His conclusion: "If we buy the [the 12 planned Ohio replacement (SSBNX) ballistic missile submarines] within existing [Navy] funds, we will not reach 300 ships. In fact, we'll find ourselves closer to 250. At these numbers, our global presence will be reduced such that we'll only be able to visit some areas of the world episodically."

Sequestration will only make the situation worse. Burke said it would cause the Navy "to both reduce procurement as well as retire existing ships, leaving us with a Navy in the vicinity of 200 ships, at which point we may not be considered a global navy."[47]

In a situation of reduced levels of defense spending, such as what would occur if defense spending were to remain constrained to the revised cap levels in the Budget Control Act, the affordability challenge posed by the 30-year shipbuilding plan would be intensified. Even then, however, the current 30-year shipbuilding plan would not necessarily become unaffordable.[48]

The Navy estimates that, in constant FY2013 dollars, fully implementing the current 30-year shipbuilding plan would require an average of $16.8 billion in annual funding for new-construction ships, compared to a historic average of $12 billion to $14 billion provided for this purpose.[49] The required increase in average annual funding of $2.8 billion to $4.8 billion per year

---

[45] *Report to Congress on the Annual Long-Range Plan for Construction of Naval Vessels for FY2014*, May 2013, pp. 11-12, 18-19.

[46] Vice Admiral Burke retired on May 20, 2013.

[47] Walter Pincus, "Budget Cuts Could Reshape Country's Ship Supply," *Washington Post*, May 2, 2013: 15.

[48] This paragraph and those that follow are adapted from Statement of Ronald O'Rourke, Specialist in Naval Affairs, Congressional Research Service, Before the House Armed Services Committee Subcommittee on Seapower and Projection Forces, on the Navy's FY2014 30-Year Shipbuilding Plan, October 23, 2013, pp. 1-4.

[49] See *Report to Congress on the Annual Long-Range Plan for Construction of Naval Vessels for FY2014*, May 2013, p. (continued...)

equates to less than 1% of DOD's annual budget under the revised caps of the Budget Control Act. CBO estimates that, in constant FY2013 dollars, fully implementing the current 30-year shipbuilding plan would require an average of $19.3 billion in annual funding for new-construction ships, or $2.5 billion per year more than the Navy estimates.[50] This would make the required increase in average annual funding $5.3 billion to $7.3 billion per year, which equates to roughly 1.1% to 1.5% of DOD's annual budget under the revised caps of the Budget Control Act.

Some observers, noting the U.S. strategic rebalancing toward the Asia-Pacific region, have advocated shifting a greater share of the DOD budget to the Navy and Air Force, on the grounds that the Asia-Pacific region is primarily a maritime and aerospace theater for DOD. In discussing the idea of shifting a greater share of the DOD budget to the Navy and Air Force, some of these observers refer to breaking the so-called "one-third, one-third, one-third" division of resources among the three military departments—a shorthand term sometimes used to refer to the more-or-less stable division of resources between the three military departments that existed for the three decades between the end of U.S. participation in the Vietnam War in 1973 and the start of the Iraq War in 2003.[51] In a context of breaking the "one-third, one-third, one-third" allocation with an aim of better aligning defense spending with the strategic rebalancing, shifting 1.5% or less of DOD's budget into the Navy's shipbuilding account would appear to be quite feasible.

More broadly, if defense spending were to remain constrained to the revised cap levels in the Budget Control Act, then fully funding the Department of the Navy's total budget at the levels shown in the current Future Years Defense Plan (FYDP) would require increasing the Department of the Navy's share of the non-Defense-Wide part of the DOD budget to about 41%, compared to about 36% in the FY2014 budget and an average of about 37% for the three-decade period between the Vietnam and Iraq wars.[52] While shifting 4% or 5% of DOD's budget to the Department of the Navy would be a more ambitious reallocation than shifting 1.5% or less of the DOD budget to the Navy's shipbuilding account, similarly large reallocations have occurred in the past:

- From the mid-1950s to the mid-1960s, reflecting a U.S. defense strategy at the time that placed a strong reliance on the deterrent value of nuclear weapons, the

---

(...continued)

18.

[50] Congressional Budget Office, *An Analysis of the Navy's Fiscal Year 2014 Shipbuilding Plan*, October 2013, Table 3 (page 13).

[51] The "one-third, one-third, one-third" terminology, though convenient, is not entirely accurate—the military departments' shares of the DOD budget, while more or less stable during this period, were not exactly one-third each: the average share for the Department of the Army was about 26%, the average share for the Department of the Navy (which includes both the Navy and Marine Corps) was about 32%, the average share for the Department of the Air Force was about 30%, and the average share for Defense-Wide (the fourth major category of DOD spending) was about 12%. Excluding the Defense-Wide category, which has grown over time, the shares for the three military departments of the remainder of DOD's budget during this period become about 29% for the Department of the Army, about 37% for the Department of the Navy, and about 34% for the Department of the Air Force.

[52] Since the Defense-Wide portion of the budget has grown from just a few percent in the 1950s and 1960s to about 15% in more recent years, including the Defense-Wide category of spending in the calculation can lead to military department shares of the budget in the 1950s and 1960s that are somewhat more elevated compared to those in more recent years, making it more complex to compare the military departments' shares across the entire period of time since the end of the World War II. For this reason, military department shares of the DOD budget cited in this statement are calculated after excluding the Defense-Wide category. The points made in this statement, however, can still made on the basis of a calculation that includes the Defense-Wide category.

Department of the Air Force's share of the non-Defense-Wide DOD budget increased by several percentage points. The Department of the Air Force's share averaged about 45% for the 10-year period FY1956-FY1965, and peaked at more than 47% in FY1957-FY1959.

- For the 11-year period FY2003-FY2013, as a consequence of combat operations in Iraq and Afghanistan, the Department of the Army's share of the non-Defense-Wide DOD budget increased by roughly 10 percentage points. The Department of the Army's share during this period averaged about 39%, and peaked at more than 43% in FY2008. U.S. combat operations in Iraq and Afghanistan during this period reflected the implementation of U.S. national strategy as interpreted by policymakers during those years.

The point of the foregoing is not to argue whether it would be right or wrong to shift more of the DOD budget to the Navy's shipbuilding account or to the Department of the Navy's budget generally. Doing that would require reducing funding for other DOD programs, and policymakers would need to weigh the resulting net impact on overall DOD capabilities. The point, rather, is to note that the allocation of DOD resources is not fixed, that aligning DOD spending with U.S. strategy in coming years could involve changing the allocation by more than a very marginal amount, and that such a changed allocation could provide the funding needed to implement the current 30-year shipbuilding plan. The alternative of assuming at the outset that there is no potential for making anything more than very marginal shifts in the allocation of DOD resources could unnecessarily constrain options available to policymakers and prevent the allocation of DOD resources from being aligned optimally with U.S. strategy.

As an alternative or supplement to the option of altering the allocation of DOD resources among the military departments, the 30-year shipbuilding plan could also become more affordable by taking actions beyond those now being implemented by DOD to control military personnel pay and benefits and reduce what some observers refer to as DOD's overhead or back-office costs. Multiple organizations have made recommendations for such actions in recent years. The Defense Business Board, for example, estimated that at least $200 billion of DOD's enacted budget for FY2010 constituted overhead costs. The board stated, "There has been an explosion of overhead work because the Department has failed to establish adequate controls to keep it in line relative to the size of the warfight," and that "in order to accomplish that work, the Department has applied ever more personnel to those tasks which has added immensely to costs." The board stated further that "whether it's improving the tooth-to-tail ratio; increasing the 'bang for the buck', or converting overhead to combat, Congress and DoD must significantly change their approach," and that DOD "must use the numerous world-class business practices and proven business operations that are applicable to DoD's overhead."[53]

One potential way to interpret the affordability challenge posed by the Navy's 30-year shipbuilding plan is to view it as an invitation by the Navy for policymakers to consider matters such as the alignment between U.S. strategy and the division of DOD resources among the

---

[53] Defense Business Board briefing, "Reducing Overhead and Improving Business Operations, Initial Observations," July 22, 2010, slides 15, 5, and 6, posted online at http://www.govexec.com/pdfs/072210rb1.pdf. See also Defense Business Board, *Modernizing the Military Retirement System*, Report to the Secretary of Defense, Report FY11-05, posted online at http://dbb.defense.gov/Portals/35/Documents/Reports/2011/FY11-5_Modernizing_The_Military_Retirement_System_2011-7.pdf; and Defense Business Board, *Corporate Downsizing Applications for DoD*, Report to the Secretary of Defense, Report FY11-08, posted online at http://dbb.defense.gov/Portals/35/Documents/Reports/2011/FY11-8_Corporate_Downsizing_Applications_for_DoD_2011-7.pdf.

military departments, and the potential for taking actions beyond those now being implemented by DOD to control military personnel pay and benefits and reduce DOD overhead and back-office costs. The Navy's prepared statement for a September 18, 2013, hearing before the House Armed Services Committee on planning for sequestration in FY2014 and the perspectives of the military services on the Strategic Choices and Management Review (SCMR) provides a number of details about reductions in Navy force structure and acquisition programs that could result from constraining DOD's budget to the revised cap levels in the Budget Control Act.[54] These potential reductions do not appear to reflect any substantial shift in the allocation of DOD resources among the military departments, or the taking of actions beyond those already being implemented by DOD to control DOD personnel pay and benefits and reduce DOD overhead and back-office costs. The fact that the Navy in its prepared statement did not choose to discuss the possibility of a changed allocation of DOD resources among the military departments or additional actions to control DOD personnel pay and benefits and reduce DOD overhead and back-office costs does not prevent Congress from considering such possibilities.

Legislative Activity for FY2014

FY2014 Funding Request

The Navy's proposed FY2014 budget requests funding for the procurement of 8 new battle force ships (i.e., ships that count against the 306-ship goal)—two Virginia-class attack submarines, one DDG-51 class Aegis destroyer, four Littoral Combat Ships (LCSs), and one Mobile Landing Platform/Afloat Forward Staging Base (MLP/AFSB) ship. These ships are all funded through the Shipbuilding and Conversion, Navy (SCN) account.

FY2014 National Defense Authorization Act (H.R. 1960/S. 1197)

House

The House Armed Services Committee, in its report (H.Rept. 113-102 of June 7, 2013) on H.R. 1960, supported the Navy's requests for funding for the procurement of 8 new battle force ships, approving, and in some cases recommending increases above, the requested amounts. (Pages 387-388) The report recommended:

- an increase of $492 million for the Virginia-class attack submarine program, which almost matches the $492.3 million sequestered from the program by the March 1, 2013, sequester (see "Impact of March 1, 2013, Sequester on FY2013 Funding" in "Oversight Issues for Congress for FY2014");

- an increase of $332 million for the DDG-51 program, which is similar to the amount of additional funding that the Navy has testified would be needed to execute the third DDG-51 procured in FY2013 (i.e., the tenth DDG-51 in the FY2013-FY2017 DDG-51 multi-year procurement contract);

---

[54] Statement of Admiral Jonathan Greenert, U.S. Navy, Chief of Naval Operations, Before the House Armed Services Committee on Planning for Sequestration in FY 2014 and Perspectives of the Military Services on the Strategic Choices and Management Review, September 18, 2013, pp. 6-10.

- an increase of $79.3 million for the DDG-1000 destroyer program, which is $9 million more than the $70.3 million sequestered from the program by the March 1, 2013, sequester;

- an increase of $23.4 million for the Moored Training Ship program, matching the amount sequestered from the program by the March 1, 2013, sequester; and

- an increase of $7.6 million for the JHSV program, which is about one-third as much as the $21.4 million sequestered from the program by the March 1, 2013, sequester.

Section 1022 of H.R. 1960 as reported states:

> SEC. 1022. AVAILABILITY OF FUNDS FOR RETIREMENT OR INACTIVATION OF TICONDEROGA CLASS CRUISERS OR DOCK LANDING SHIPS.
>
> (a) Limitation on Availability of Funds-
>
> (1) IN GENERAL- Except as provided in paragraph (2), none of the funds authorized to be appropriated by this Act or otherwise made available for fiscal year 2014 for the Department of Defense may be obligated or expended to retire, prepare to retire, inactivate, or place in storage a cruiser or dock landing ship.
>
> (2) EXCEPTION- Notwithstanding paragraph (1), the funds referred to in such subsection may be obligated or expended to retire the U.S.S. Denver, LPD9.
>
> (b) Authority to Transfer Authorizations-
>
> (1) AUTHORITY- Subject to the availability of appropriations for such purpose, the Secretary of Defense may transfer amounts of authorizations made available to the Department of Defense for fiscal year 2013 specifically for the modernization of vessels referred to in subsection (a)(1). Amounts of authorizations so transferred shall be merged with and be available for the same purposes as the authorization to which transferred.
>
> (2) LIMITATION- The total amount of authorizations that the Secretary may transfer under the authority of this subsection may not exceed $914,676,000.
>
> (3) ADDITIONAL AUTHORITY- The transfer authority provided by this subsection is in addition to the transfer authority provided under section 1001 of this Act and under section 1001 of the National Defense Authorization Act for Fiscal Year 2013 (P.L. 112-239; 126 Stat. 1902).

Regarding Section 1022, H.Rept. 113-102 states:

> Section 1022—Availability of Funds for Retirement or Inactivation of Ticonderoga Class Cruisers or Dock Landing Ships
>
> This section would limit the obligation and expenditure of funds authorized to be appropriated or otherwise made available for fiscal year 2014 for the retirement, inactivation, or storage of a cruiser or dock landing ship. This section would provide an exception for the retirement of the U.S.S. Denver (LPD 9).
>
> This section would further provide for transfer authority for the purpose of providing sufficient appropriations to support the modernization of seven cruisers. If requested by the

Secretary of Defense, the committee believes the following transfers should be included: OPN Line 0960, $662.7 million; OPN Line 2312, $1.8 million; OPN Line 2360, $6.6 million; OPN Line 2915, $13.7 million; OPN Line 3050, $13.4 million; OPN Line 3216, $20.8 million; OPN Line 5530, $4.6 million; WPN Line 4223, $91.1 million; and RDTE Line 1447, $100.0 million. The total transfer authority is $914.7 million. (Pages 233-234)

Section 1024 states:

SEC. 1024. SENSE OF CONGRESS REGARDING A BALANCED FUTURE NAVAL FORCE.

(a) Findings- Congress makes the following findings:

(1) The battle force of the Navy must be sufficiently sized and balanced in capability to meet current and anticipated future national security objectives.

(2) A robust and balanced naval force is required for the Department of Defense to fully execute the President's National Security Strategy.

(3) To develop and sustain required capabilities the Navy must balance investment and maintenance costs across various ship types, including—

(A) aircraft carriers;

(B) surface combatants;

(C) submarines;

(D) amphibious assault ships; and

(E) other auxiliary vessels, including support vessels operated by the Military Sealift Command.

(4) Despite a Marine Corps requirement for 38 amphibious assault ships, the Navy possesses only 30 amphibious assault ships with an average of 22 ships available for surge deployment.

(5) The inadequate level of investment in Navy shipbuilding over the last 20 years has resulted in—

(A) a fragile shipbuilding industrial base, both in the construction yards and secondary suppliers of materiel and equipment; and

(B) increased costs per vessel stemming from low production volume.

(6) The Department of Defense, Military Construction and Veterans Affairs, and Full-Year Continuing Appropriations Act for Fiscal Year 2013 provided $263,000,000 towards the advance procurement of materiel and equipment required to continue the San Antonio LPD 17 amphibious transport dock class to a total of 12 ships, a key first step in rebalancing the amphibious assault ship force structure.

(b) Sense of Congress- It is the Sense of Congress that—

(1) the Department of Defense and the Department of the Navy must prioritize funding towards increased shipbuilding rates to enable the Navy to meet the full-range of combatant commander requests;

(2) the Department of the Navy's future budget requests and the Long Range Plan for the Construction of Naval Forces must realistically anticipate and reflect the true investment necessary to meet stated force structure goals;

(3) without modification to Long Range Plan for the Construction of Naval Forces shipbuilding plan, the future of the industrial base that enables construction of large, combat-survivable amphibious assault ships is at significant risk; and

(4) the Department of Defense and Congress should act expeditiously to restore the force structure and capability balance of the Navy fleet as quickly as possible.

Regarding Section 1024, H.Rept. 113-102 states:

> Section 1024—Sense of Congress Regarding a Balanced Future Naval Force

> This section would provide the Sense of Congress that additional funding should be prioritized toward shipbuilding efforts and that Department of Navy budget projections should realistically anticipate the true investment to meet force structure goals. (Page 234)

Section 1233 states:

> SEC. 1233. SENSE OF CONGRESS ON THE DEFENSE OF THE ARABIAN GULF.

> (a) Findings- Congress finds the following:

> (1) In response to U.S. Central Command requirements, the United States Navy has maintained, on average, more than one aircraft carrier in the Arabian Gulf for more than five years.

> (2) In February 2013, the senior leadership of the Department of Defense elected to reduce the number of aircraft carriers deployed to the Arabian Gulf in light of budget constraints and limitation of the overall carrier force structure to support the two aircraft carrier requirement.

> (3) In reference to the decision to indefinitely delay the deployment of the USS Harry Truman, CVN 75, and the USS Gettysburg, its cruiser escort, Chairman of the Joint Chiefs, General Martin Dempsey stated, `We're trying to stretch our readiness out by keeping this particular carrier in homeport in our global response force, so if something happens elsewhere in the world, we can respond to it. Had we deployed it and `consumed' that readiness, we could have created a situation where downstream we wouldn't have a carrier present in certain parts of the world at all.'.

> (4) Highlighting the risks of having only one aircraft carrier in the region and relying on land-based aircraft, General Dempsey stated, `When you have carrier-based aircraft, you have complete autonomy and control over when you use them. When you use land-based aircraft, you often have to have host-nation permission to use them.'.

> (5) Addressing the perception of the United States commitment to the region, General James Mattis, Commander of U.S. Central Command, testified in March 2013, `Perhaps the greatest risk to U.S. interests in the region is a perceived lack of an enduring U.S. commitment to collective interests and the security of our regional partners.'. He went on to

testify that, `The drawdown of our forces can be misinterpreted as a lack of attention, a lack of commitment to the region.'.

(b) Sense of Congress- It is the sense of Congress that—

(1) maintaining only one aircraft carrier battle group in the Arabian Gulf constrains United States' options and could put at risk the ability to have diversified platforms from which to defend the Arabian Gulf and, if necessary, to conduct military operations to prevent Iran from threatening the United States, United States allies, or Iran's neighbors with nuclear weapons;

(2) it is in the interests of the United States to maintain both land-based and sea-based capabilities in the region to project force;

(3) land-based locations in the region could restrict United States military options and critically impact the operational capability if required to conduct a defense of the Arabian Gulf because the United States has not finalized bilateral security agreements with key Gulf Cooperation Council countries;

(4) as a result of these and other critical limitations associated with maintaining one aircraft carrier battle group in the Arabian Gulf, United States military commanders have expressed concerns about the operational constraints, the increasing uncertainty among United States allies, and the emboldening of potential adversaries such as Iran;

(5) regarding the ability of the United States Navy to maintain a two aircraft carrier presence in the Arabian Gulf, the Chief of Naval Operations, Admiral Jonathan Greenert, stated, `We need 11 carriers to do the job. That's been pretty clearly written, and that's underwritten in our defense strategic guidance.'.

(6) the United States should construct and sufficiently sustain a fleet of at least eleven aircraft carriers and associated battle force ships in order to meet current and future requirements and to support at least a two aircraft carrier battle group presence in the Arabian Gulf, in addition to meeting other operational requirements; and

(7) the United States should finalize bilateral agreements with key Gulf Cooperation Council countries that support the Defense of the Arabian Gulf requirements, at the earliest possible date.

Regarding Section 1233, H.Rept. 113-102 states:

Section 1233—Sense of Congress on the Defense of the Arabian Gulf

This section would express the sense of Congress with respect to the United States' operational posture and capacity to defend the Arabian Gulf, including the risk of maintaining only 1 aircraft carrier battle group in the Arabian Gulf to deter the Government of the Islamic Republic of Iran, and the limitations on maintaining a 2 aircraft carrier battle group presence in the Arabian Gulf, stemming in part from not constructing and sustaining a fleet of at least 11 aircraft carriers. Additionally, this section would express the sense of Congress that the United States should finalize bilateral security agreements with key Gulf Cooperation Council countries that support the Defense of the Arabian Gulf requirements at the earliest possible date. (Page 273)

H.Rept. 113-102 also states:

The committee is concerned about the Navy's overall fleet size and the continuous sustained demand for naval forces, especially in light of the Administration's strategic shift to operations in the Asia-Pacific. Therefore, the restriction precluding the Navy from retiring seven Ticonderoga-class guided missile cruisers and two amphibious ships well before the end of their expected service life continues for fiscal year 2014. The committee would provide additional funds to the Navy to properly modernize and maintain these critical naval assets. The committee notes that it is less costly to maintain existing assets than to procure new ones and this funding ensures the correct naval capabilities and fleet mix for the length of time originally authorized by Congress....

The committee also would fund needed ship construction to obviate the negative consequences of sequestration on the various ship construction programs. The committee would provide sufficient funds to support the acquisition of the 10th DDG–51 class destroyer of a multiyear procurement; additional funds to support the continued acquisition of two Virginia Class attack submarines; and additional funds associated with the completion of the DDG–1000 class destroyer, the Moored Training Ship, and the Joint High Speed Vessel. (Page 6)

H.Rept. 113-102 also states:

Long-range plan for the construction of naval vessels

Pursuant to section 231 of title 10, United States Code, the Secretary of Defense provided the annual long-range plan for the construction of naval vessels on May 10, 2013, as informed by the Future Years Defense Program (FYDP) for fiscal years 2014–18. The Secretary also indicated that a force structure of "about 300 ships" would be necessary to support ongoing naval operations. The Secretary further highlights the "resourcing challenges outside the FYDP largely due to investment requirements associated with the SSBN(X) program". The Secretary acknowledges that these ship construction pressures will precipitate higher fiscal requirements in the mid-term planning period (fiscal years 2024–33) requiring an annual investment of $19.8 billion per year in fiscal year 2013 constant dollars.

The committee supports a robust shipbuilding plan that invests in the near and long term needs of our Navy, and considers the recapitalization of the SSBN fleet a challenging but necessary strategic priority. However, the committee is concerned that the Navy's ship construction accounts will face significant pressure in supporting long term ship requirements while also resourcing the Ohio-class replacement ballistic missile submarine program. The committee also believes that a significant increase to the ship construction accounts is unsustainable in times of budget challenges.

The Congressional Budget Office has estimated that the average ship construction investment over the last 30 years, in current dollars, is $16.0 billion. Therefore, to better understand the significance associated with even sustaining the current ship construction investment throughout the long-range plan, the committee directs the Secretary of the Navy to provide a report to the congressional defense committee by March 1, 2014, that provides an update to the long plan for the construction of naval vessels based on $16.0 billion across the entirety of the long-range plan and to assess the corresponding reductions in the shipbuilding plan. The Secretary of the Navy should also provide an assessment of this investment in terms of the health associated with the industrial base, as well as a discussion of alternative strategies for the Navy and Congress to consider in alleviating any shortfalls between this assessment and the May 10 report. (Page 29)

Senate

The Senate Armed Services Committee, in its report (S.Rept. 113-44 of June 20, 2013) on S. 1197, supported the Navy's requests for funding for the procurement of 8 new battle force ships, approving, and in two cases recommending increases above, the requested amounts. (Pages 295-296) The report recommended:

- an increase of $100 million for the DDG-51 program, to "Help buy [a] 3rd DDG–51 in FY[20]13;" and

- an increase of $55.3 million for the Afloat Forward Staging Base (AFSB) program, reflecting a "Navy requested adjustment."

Section 1021 of S. 1197 as reported states:

> SEC. 1021. MODIFICATION OF REQUIREMENTS FOR ANNUAL LONG-RANGE PLAN FOR THE CONSTRUCTION OF NAVAL VESSELS.
>
> (a) Annual Naval Vessel Construction Plan- Subsection (b) of section 231 of title 10, United States Code, is amended—
>
> (1) in paragraph (1)—
>
> (A) by striking `should be designed' both places it appears and inserting `shall be designed';
> and
>
> (B) by striking `is capable of supporting' both places it appears and inserting `supports'; and
>
> (2) in paragraph (2)—
>
> (A) in subparagraph (B), by inserting `and capabilities' after `naval vessel force structure';
> and
>
> (B) by adding at the end the following new subparagraph:
>
> `(D) The estimated total cost of construction for each vessel used to determine estimated levels of annual funding under subparagraph (C).'.
>
> (b) Assessment When Construction Plan Does Not Meet Force Structure Requirements- Such section is further amended—
>
> (1) by redesignating subsections (d), (e), and (f) as subsections (e), (f), and (g), respectively;
> and
>
> (2) by inserting after subsection (c) the following new subsection (d):
>
> `(d) Assessment When Annual Naval Vessel Construction Plan Does Not Meet Force Structure Requirements- If the annual naval vessel construction plan for a fiscal year under subsection (b) does not result in a force structure or capabilities that meet the requirements identified in subsection (b)(2)(B), the Secretary shall include with the defense budget materials for that fiscal year an assessment of the extent of the strategic and operational risk to national security associated with the reduced force structure of naval vessels over the period of time that the required force structure or capabilities are not achieved. Such assessment shall include an analysis whether the risks are acceptable, and plans to mitigate

such risks. Such assessment shall be coordinated in advance with the commanders of the combatant commands and the Nuclear Weapons Council under section 179 of this title.'.

Regarding Section 1021, S.Rept. 113-44 states:

Modification of requirements for annual long-range plan for the construction of naval vessels (sec. 1021)

The committee recommends a provision that would modify section 231 of title 10, Unites Sates Code, to include a requirement to report on the total cost of construction for each vessel used to determine estimated levels of annual funding in the report, and an assessment of the extent of the strategic and operational risk to national security whenever the number or capabilities of the naval vessels in the plan do not meet requirements. (Page 172)

Section 1022 states:

SEC. 1022. REPORT ON NAVAL VESSELS AND THE FORCE STRUCTURE ASSESSMENT.

(a) Report Required- Not later than February 1, 2014, the Chief of Naval Operations shall submit to the congressional defense committees a report on current and anticipated requirements for combatant vessels of the Navy over the next 30 years.

(b) Elements- The report required by subsection (a) shall include the following:

(1) A description of the naval capability requirements identified by the combatant commands in developing the Force Structure Assessment (FSA) in 2005 and revalidating that Assessment in 2010.

(2) The capabilities for each class of vessel that was assumed in the Force Structure Assessment.

(3) An assessment of the capabilities of the current fleet of combatant vessels of the Navy to meet current and anticipated requirements.

(4) An assessment the capabilities of the anticipated fleet of combatant vessels of the Navy to meet emerging threats over the next 30 years.

(5) An assessment of how the Navy will meet combatant command requirements for forward-deployed naval capabilities with a smaller number of ships and submarines.

(6) An assessment of how the Navy will manage the risk of massing a greater set of capabilities on a smaller number of ships while facing an expanding range of asymmetrical threats, such as—

(A) anti-access/area-denial capabilities;

(B) diesel-electric submarines;

(C) mines; and

(D) anti-ship cruise and ballistic missiles.

(c) Form- The report required by subsection (a) shall be submitted in unclassified form, but may include a classified annex.

Regarding Section 1022, S.Rept. 113-44 states:

Report on naval vessels and the Force Structure Assessment (sec. 1022)

The committee recommends a provision that would direct the Chief of Naval Operations (CNO) to provide a report to the congressional defense committees no later than February 1, 2014, that would assess the current fleet capabilities compared to the threat and the likely situation over the next 30 years. The CNO should produce an unclassified report, and a classified annex to that report.

Section 1105 of the National Defense Authorization Act for Fiscal Year 2013 (Public Law 112–239) required the Secretary of the Navy to provide a comprehensive description of the current requirements for combatant vessels of the Navy, including submarines. The Navy submitted that report which reflected that, while the previous requirement was for a fleet of 313 ships, originally identified in a 2005 Force Structure Assessment (FSA) and revalidated in 2010, the new requirements have declined to a total of 306 ships.

Within this seven-ship net decrease to 306 ships, actual combat power is reduced by six large surface combatants, three small surface combatants, and four cruise missile submarines, for a total reduction of 13 combatant ships, offset by an increase of six command and support ships. The reduction in cruise missile submarines reflects a Navy plan not to replace these ships when they retire in the late 2020s.

In congressional testimony this year about the 2012 FSA, representatives of the Department of the Navy asserted that the revised fleet size goal considered various factors, including the revised Defense Strategic Guidance in 2012, changed Navy mission requirements, different individual ship capabilities, fleet networking capabilities, and ship basing arrangements and operational cycles, as opposed to just platforms or numbers of ships.

The committee notes that the current fleet of 283 battle force ships provides combatant commanders (COCOM) with a greater array of fire power than did the Navy fleets of 500 or more ships of the Cold War era, with precision-guided air-delivered weapons, numbers of Tomahawk-capable ships, and the sophistication of command, control, communications, and computer systems; intelligence, surveillance, and reconnaissance (ISR) systems; and networking capabilities that did not exist during the Cold War.

The President's 2012 revised U.S. defense strategy calls for a rebalancing towards the Asia-Pacific region, a predominantly maritime and aerospace domain. This will most likely increase demands for Navy fleet resources and deployments in that region in competition with global demand. Regarding global demands for naval forces, Navy officials testified last year that fully satisfying COCOM requests for forward-deployed Navy forces in various regions would require more than 500 ships.

The Report to Congress on the Annual Long-Range Plan for Construction of Naval Vessels for FY 2014, dated May 10, 2013, proposes near-term retirements of cruisers and amphibious ships, resulting in 270 ships, the smallest fleet since 1917. The committee is concerned that the plan will not meet the goal of a 306-ship battle force inventory until 2037 and assumes risk over the 30-year period, with periodic shortages of aircraft carriers, cruisers, destroyers, attack submarines, and amphibious ships. The committee notes that the Navy possesses only 28 amphibious ships, with an average of only 22 ships available for surge deployment, despite a Marine Corps requirement for 38 amphibious ships. As such, the committee is also concerned that the Navy's shortfall in amphibious ships adds risk to the Marine Corps' ability to meet current and future COCOM requests.

There are also risks with the Navy's plan beyond mere numbers of ships:

(1) within the plan, the Navy intends that the Littoral Combat Ship (LCS) will comprise over one third of the Navy's total surface combatant fleet by 2028. This fact compounds risk, since the LCS to date has not completed operational testing or demonstrated adequate performance of assigned missions in critical areas of mine countermeasures, anti-surface warfare, or anti-submarine operations;

(2) with its decision in the fiscal year 2013 budget to delay the procurement of the first Ohio-class replacement ballistic missile submarine by 2 years, to fiscal year 2021, the Navy has consumed all schedule margin for replacing the existing Ohio-class boats on a timely basis, and increased the risk that an unforeseen event affecting a strategic missile submarine's operational availability would prevent the Navy from being able to fully satisfy U.S. Strategic Command (STRATCOM) requirements; and

(3) the 2012 FSA and the shipbuilding plan do not account for the possible effects of further budget cuts under the Budget Control Act of 2011. Various representatives of the Navy have testified that, if Department of Defense budgets are reduced below levels shown in the President's budget request for fiscal year 2014, the Navy will have to reduce the size and capabilities of the fleet to reflect further changes in U.S. defense strategy and available Navy resources.

Given the risks inherent in the planned size of the Navy, the capabilities of the ships planned, the rate of Navy ship procurement, and the potential affordability of the Navy's shipbuilding plans at a time of significant uncertainty in defense budgets, the committee agrees that in order to adequately assess the ability of the fleet proposed by the 2012 FSA to meet national security requirements, there needs to be an objective set of standards to assess the ability of the Navy to meet national security objectives, as opposed to simply relying on numbers and types of platforms.

The committee also believes that a failure to recapitalize our seabased strategic nuclear deterrent on time would have devastating impacts on deterrence and strategic stability. Accordingly, the committee directs the CNO to pay particular attention in producing the report to the Navy's ability to fully meet STRATCOM requirements. (Pages 172-174)

Section 1023 states:

SEC. 1023. REPEAL OF POLICY RELATING TO PROPULSION SYSTEMS OF ANY NEW CLASS OF MAJOR COMBATANT VESSELS OF THE STRIKE FORCES OF THE UNITED STATES NAVY.

Section 1012 of the National Defense Authorization Act for Fiscal Year 2008 (10 U.S.C. 7291 note) is repealed.

Regarding Section 1023, S.Rept. 113-44 states:

Repeal of policy relating to propulsion systems of any new class of major combatant vessels of the strike forces of the United States Navy (sec. 1023)

The committee recommends a provision that would repeal section 1012 of the National Defense Authorization Act for Fiscal Year 2008 (Public Law 110–181). That section requires that the Navy build any new class of major surface combatant and amphibious assault ship with an integrated nuclear power system, unless the Secretary of the Navy notifies the congressional defense committees that, as a result of a cost-benefit analysis, it would not be practical for the Navy to design the class of ships with an integrated nuclear power system.

As a matter of acquisition management laws and regulations, the Navy must conduct an analysis of alternatives (AoA) for all such vessels to determine the ship characteristics, including the required propulsion and power generation mechanism. The AoA outcome for each surface combatant and amphibious assault ship should be based on an independent and objective systems engineering and business case analysis. Within that analysis, the Navy can evaluate the advisability of using an integrated nuclear propulsion system to determine the best value for the Federal Government. (Pages 174-175)

S.Rept. 113-44 also states:

Ship Modernization, Operations and Sustainment Fund

Section 8105 of the Defense Appropriations Act for Fiscal Year 2013 (Public Law 113–6) established the Ship Modernization, Operations and Sustainment Fund, and appropriated more than $2.4 billion to the Fund. The Fund was intended to prevent the premature retirement of seven cruisers and two dock landing ships during fiscal years 2013 and 2014. This reflected a concern with the proposed retirement plan that the plan: (1) was disconnected from the defense strategy; (2) created future unaffordable shipbuilding requirements; and (3) would exacerbate force structure shortfalls that negatively impact the Department's ability to meet combatant commander (COCOM) requirements.

The Report to Congress on the Annual Long-Range Plan for Construction of Naval Vessels for fiscal year 2014, date May 10, 2013, proposes to retire these cruisers and amphibious ships during fiscal year 2015, resulting in a fleet of 270 ships, the smallest fleet since 1917. The Navy is taking this action despite the fact that keeping these vessels operating until the end of 2014 will cost, according to the Navy, $931.1 million. The committee believes that the Navy should use the remaining resources in the Fund to sustain all of these ships. Available funds would permit the Navy to operate the ships during most of the period future-years defense program and would permit the Navy and Congress to continue evaluating options for modernizing and retaining these vessels until the end of their expected service lives. (Pages 30-31)

S.Rept. 113-44 also states:

LHA–8 design effort

The budget request included $155.3 million in PE [Program Element] 64567N for various ship design and research and development efforts, including $30.8 million for the next amphibious assault ship, LHA–8. Within the $30.8 million, $14.5 million is for LHA–8 ship design. Navy LHA–8 program development and design activities have involved two shipyards, among other contractors. The Navy intends to begin procurement funding for LHA–8 in fiscal year 2015.

Repeated Navy shipbuilding programs have shown that failing to complete a ship's design before starting construction inevitably leads to cost growth and schedule delays. The committee believes that the Navy should invest more than it is currently planning to invest in maturing the design of LHA–8 before starting construction activities.

Therefore, the committee recommends an increase of $20.0 million in PE 64567N for maturing the LHA–8 design. (Page 44-45)

FY2014 DOD Appropriations Act (H.R. 2397/S. 1429)

House

The House Appropriations Committee, in its report (H.Rept. 113-113 of June 17, 2013) on H.R. 2397, generally supported the Navy's requests for funding for the procurement of 8 new battle force ships while recommending increases and reductions to some of the requested amounts. (Pages 163-164) The report recommended:

- a $950 million increase to the Virginia class submarine program to "Fully fund the Virginia class submarine program;"

- a $96.1 million reduction to the program for performing mid-life nuclear refueling overhauls on existing Nimitz (CVN-68) class carriers for an "Asset due to prior year above threshold reprogramming;"

- a $38 million increase for the Afloat Forward Staging Base (AFSB) program for "Program shortfall;"

- a $23.4 million increase for the Moored Training Ship program for "Program shortfall," matching the amount sequestered from the program by the March 1, 2013, sequester; and

- a $7.6 million increase for the JHSV program for "Program shortfall," which is about one-third as much as the $21.4 million sequestered from the program by the March 1, 2013, sequester.

H.Rept. 113-113 states:

SHIPBUILDING

Despite assurances from the Navy that the shipbuilding account is as healthy as it has ever been, the Committee remains skeptical. The Navy's new stated required fleet size is 306 ships, down from the long stated but never achieved fleet size of 313 ships. The annual 30 year shipbuilding report provided by the Navy shows that the fleet will reach the required fleet size of 306 ships in the year 2037, a full quarter century from now. The Secretary of the Navy testified that the fleet size will reach the 300 ship mark by the end of the decade. While this is encouraging, the Committee is concerned the fleet size remains at 300 ships for a single year, then drops back under 300 until 2024. In fact, of the 30 years that comprise the plan, the fleet size is under 300 ships for 16 of these years. The fleet size is at the required 306 ships or above for only the final seven years (2037 to 2043) that are displayed in the report. The Committee believes a truly healthy shipbuilding program should reach and sustain the required fleet size sooner than the Navy is projecting.

Additionally, the Navy requested authority to incrementally fund a Virginia Class Submarine in fiscal year 2014. The Congress has authorized and appropriated funding for 18 fully funded Virginia Class Submarines in the years prior to fiscal year 2014. The Committee does not understand why funding requested for this particular submarine requires violating the Department of Defense's long standing full funding policy. The Committee is puzzled by Navy claims of billions of dollars in savings for the taxpayers as it is the Committee's understanding that these savings come from the fact that the program is conducting a multi-year procurement of ten submarines and not from the fact that one of the submarines is incrementally funded. Quality budget discipline, not funding gimmicks, is called for more than ever in these times of decreasing budgets and budget uncertainty.

Contributing to the poor health of the shipbuilding program is sequestration. As a direct result of sequestration, a minimum of seven destroyers and submarines from fiscal year 2013 and prior years are no longer fully funded. The cost to make the funding for these ships whole is just over $1,000,000,000. This funding will be required in the outyears to complete the construction of these ships. When this funding is added to the funding required to complete the incrementally funded submarine, the cost to complete these ships is in excess of $2,000,000,000. This represents funding that will not be available to purchase new equipment or increase readiness in future years, because it will have to pay the debt incurred by the Navy in years past. While sequestration is in statute, the Committee is extremely concerned about the Navy willfully adding to its outyear liabilities by incrementally funding a submarine. Therefore, the recommendation provides an additional $950,000,000 to the Virginia Class Submarine program to fully fund the program. Additionally, the Secretary of the Navy is directed to utilize the fiscal year 2015 funding currently reserved for the completion of the submarine to fully fund the ships and programs that were impacted by the sequestration reductions.

JOINT HIGH SPEED VESSEL

The Committee encourages the Secretary of the Navy to continue to explore missions and projects that leverage the flexibility of the Joint High Speed Vessel and explore the extension of the current mission envelope beyond in-theater transport, to include such capabilities as unmanned aerial systems and air surveillance.

SHIP DECOMMISSIONINGS

The Committee is extremely disappointed in the Navy's inaction with respect to the seven cruisers and two amphibious ships that were proposed for decommissioning in the fiscal year 2013 budget. Despite very clear direction from all four congressional defense committees to keep these ships in the fleet, the Navy has taken no steps that would indicate it is moving toward keeping the ships for the long term. The ships have significant life remaining and are less expensive to keep when compared to procuring new ships with similar capabilities. Last year the Congress provided sufficient funding for the operation and modernization of these ships through the end of fiscal year 2014 and that funding has gone largely untouched, indicating an unwillingness to commit to keep these ships in the fleet. The Committee fails to understand why the Navy would choose to decommission these ships when it is having such a difficult time maintaining the required fleet size through new procurements.

Therefore, the Committee recommendation rescinds all modernization funding from the fiscal year 2013 Ship Modernization, Operations, and Sustainment Fund and re-appropriates the funding in the Other Procurement, Navy, Weapons Procurement, Navy, and Research, Development, Test and Evaluation, Navy accounts. The Secretary of the Navy is directed to use this funding for the purpose of modernization of these seven cruisers and two amphibious ships and to retain them in the fleet. (Pages 165-166)

Senate

The Senate Appropriations Committee, in its report (S.Rept. 113-85 of August 1, 2013) on S. 1429, generally supported the Navy's requests for funding for the procurement of eight new battle force ships while recommending increases and reductions to some of the requested amounts. (Pages 100-101) The report recommended:

- a $27.313 million reduction to the CVN-78 aircraft carrier program for "Restoring acquisition accountability: Reduction in change orders" ($16.2 million) and "Maintaining program affordability: SEWIP [Surface Electronic Warfare Improvement Program] Block 3 excessive cost growth" ($11.113 million);

- a $22.1 million reduction to the program for performing mid-life nuclear refueling overhauls on existing Nimitz (CVN-68) class carriers for an "Improving funds management: CVN 72 requirement previously funded in Fiscal Year 2012 reprogramming";

- a $227 million increase to the Virginia class attack submarine program for "Maintain critical industrial base: Virginia class submarine";

- a $91 million net increase to the DDG-51 destroyer program, consisting of a $100 million increase for "Authorization adjustment: DDG–51" and a $9 million reduction for "Restoring acquisition accountability: Flight III Advance Planning early to need";

- a $55.3 million increase for the Afloat Forward Staging Base (AFSB) program for "Improving funds management: Transfer from NDSF [National Defense Sealift Fund], line 020, for full funding of ASFB #2 only, per Navy request";

- a $23.4 million increase for the Moored Training Ship program for "Improving funds management: Program shortfall, funds transferred per Navy request"; and

- a $7.6 million increase to the Joint High Speed Vessel (JHSV) program for "Improving funds management: JHSV program shortfall, funds transferred per Navy request."

S.Rept. 113-85 states:

> *Amphibious-class Warship Construction.*—The Committee notes that the fiscal year 2014 budget request submitted by the Navy, once again, failed to present a plan to address the amphibious lift shortfall that exists today. In January 2009, the Navy and Marine Corps determined a minimum force of 33 ships is the limit of acceptable risk in meeting a 38-ship amphibious warship force requirement. As of now, there are 28 ships in the Navy's amphibious fleet, with an average of only 22 ships operationally available at any given time due to maintenance and overhaul schedules. This level of assumed risk with amphibious lift capability by the Department of the Navy deeply concerns the Committee. Of particular concern is the impact it has on the ability of Commanders to meet operations plans and crisis response requirements, particularly as instability in the Middle East continues and as the Department of Defense rebalances its global posture towards the Asia-Pacific region.
>
> The ability to address the amphibious lift shortfall is exacerbated when the Navy funds only one amphibious class warship in the current 5-year Future Years Defense Program. This lack of commitment and funding by the Navy will not only have a negative impact on meeting future operations plans and crisis response requirements, but it will also have a negative industrial base impact and lead to additional cost growth in multiple shipbuilding programs. Therefore, the Committee directs the Secretary of the Navy to provide a more responsible amphibious warship acquisition plan to Congress with the fiscal year 2015 budget submission.

DDG–51 Destroyer.—The Committee understands that the DDG–51 program has a $304,000,000 shortfall due to prior year sequestration reductions, and recommends an additional $100,000,000 for the DDG–51 to allow the Navy to award the tenth DDG–51 under the current multi-year procurement contract, as previously authorized and appropriated. The Committee understands that its fiscal year 2014 shipbuilding recommendations create an outyear asset for the Navy to apply to shortfalls.

Joint High Speed Vessel.—The Committee recommends that the Navy continue to explore missions and projects that leverage the flexibility of the Joint High Speed Vessel [JHSV] and extend the mission envelope beyond in-theatre transport, including considering the addition of an unmanned aerial system and air surveillance capability to the JHSV. (Pages 101-102)

S.Rept. 113-85 also states:

SHIP MODERNIZATION, OPERATIONS AND SUSTAINMENT FUND

With the fiscal year 2014 budget submission, the Navy again proposes to prematurely retire seven Ticonderoga-class guided missile cruisers and two amphibious dock landing ships that have a combined remaining service life of over 100 years. The Committee notes that this proposal was rejected by the Congress in the Fiscal Year 2013 National Defense Authorization Act and the Fiscal Year 2013 Department of Defense Appropriations Act; and that Congress provided significant funds to man, operate, sustain and modernize these ships. As previously expressed in Senate Report 112–196, the Committee is concerned with this proposed elimination of force structure and believes it is disconnected from the strategic shift to the Asia-Pacific, creates future unaffordable shipbuilding requirements, and exacerbates force structure shortfalls that negatively impact the Department's ability to meet Combatant Command requirements.

The Committee notes that some key assumptions that led the Navy to propose prematurely retiring these ships have changed. This includes the material condition of at least one ship being superior to what the Navy assumed, as well as the scope and cost of modernization efforts required for these platforms to maintain their operational relevance for the balance of their service lives. The Committee believes that further adjustments to projected modernization efforts could be made, resulting in cost savings while retaining valuable operational capability in the near-term.

Therefore, the Committee again recommends denying these proposed premature retirements and retaining this force structure in its entirety. The Committee recommends $2,422,400,000, to man, operate, sustain, upgrade and modernize only CG–63, CG–64, CG–65, CG–66, CG–68, CG–69, CG–73, LSD–41 and LSD–46 in the Ship Modernization, Operations and Sustainment Fund, as specified elsewhere in this act. Recognizing the time required to plan and execute shipyard availabilities and modernization periods, the Committee makes these funds available until September 30, 2021. However, the Committee also believes that upgrades to these ships have been delayed for too long, and therefore directs the Secretary of the Navy to upgrade at least one of the above listed Ticonderoga-class cruisers starting in fiscal year 2014. The Committee believes that this recommendation provides the fiscal relief required by the Navy to maintain this critical force structure and allows the Navy sufficient time to budget for this force structure in future budget submissions. (Page 10)

Funding for the Ship Modernization, Operations and Sustainment Fund is provided by **Section 8102** of S. 1429 as reported by the committee. The text of Section 8102 is as follows:

Sec. 8102. (a) Of the funds previously appropriated for the `Ship Modernization, Operations and Sustainment Fund', $2,098,000,000 is hereby rescinded;

(b) There is appropriated $2,422,400,000 for the `Ship Modernization, Operations and Sustainment Fund', to remain available until September 30, 2021: Provided, That the Secretary of the Navy shall transfer funds from the `Ship Modernization, Operations and Sustainment Fund' to appropriations for military personnel; operation and maintenance; research, development, test and evaluation; and procurement, only for the purposes of manning, operating, sustaining, equipping and modernizing the Ticonderoga-class guided missile cruisers CG-63, CG-64, CG-65, CG-66, CG-68, CG-69, CG-73, and the Whidbey Island-class dock landing ships LSD-41 and LSD-46: Provided further, That funds transferred shall be merged with and be available for the same purposes and for the same time period as the appropriation to which they are transferred: Provided further, That the transfer authority provided herein shall be in addition to any other transfer authority available to the Department of Defense: Provided further, That the Secretary of the Navy shall, not less than 30 days prior to making any transfer from the `Ship Modernization, Operations and Sustainment Fund', notify the congressional defense committees in writing of the details of such transfer: Provided further, That the Secretary of the Navy shall transfer and obligate funds from the `Ship Modernization, Operations and Sustainment Fund' for modernization of not less than one Ticonderoga-class guided missile cruiser as detailed above in fiscal year 2014.

Concerning the Navy's research and development account, S.Rept. 113-85 states:

LHA 8 Amphibious Assault Ship.—The fiscal year 2014 budget request includes $19,967,000 [in research and development funding] for LHA 8 amphibious assault ship preliminary design efforts. The Committee is aware that the Department of the Navy plans to reintroduce a well deck and optimize the aviation capability of LHA 8, which is planned for initial procurement funding in fiscal year 2015. As described in the Senate report accompanying S. 1197, the National Defense Act for Fiscal Year 2014, as reported, previous Navy efforts to start ship construction prior to completing a ship's design inevitably led to cost growth and schedule delays. Considering growing fiscal pressure on the national defense budget and increasing amphibious assault ship demands from combatant commanders for contingency operations, theater security cooperation, humanitarian assistance, and conventional deterrence missions, the Committee believes it is essential that LHA 8 be introduced in the most cost-effective manner. Therefore, the Committee includes an additional $50,000,000 for LHA 8 advance planning and design and directs the Department of the Navy to work with industry to identify affordability and producibility strategies that will lead to more efficient construction of a large deck amphibious assault ship. (Pages 161-162)

CRS Reports Tracking Legislation on Specific Navy Shipbuilding Programs

For funding levels and legislative activity on individual Navy shipbuilding programs, see the following CRS reports:

- CRS Report RS20643, *Navy Ford (CVN-78) Class Aircraft Carrier Program: Background and Issues for Congress*, by Ronald O'Rourke.

- CRS Report R41129, *Navy Ohio Replacement (SSBN[X]) Ballistic Missile Submarine Program: Background and Issues for Congress*, by Ronald O'Rourke.

- CRS Report RL32418, *Navy Virginia (SSN-774) Class Attack Submarine Procurement: Background and Issues for Congress*, by Ronald O'Rourke.

- CRS Report RL32109, *Navy DDG-51 and DDG-1000 Destroyer Programs: Background and Issues for Congress*, by Ronald O'Rourke.

- CRS Report RL33741, *Navy Littoral Combat Ship (LCS) Program: Background and Issues for Congress*, by Ronald O'Rourke.

Appendix A. 2012 Testimony on Size of Navy Needed to Fully Meet COCOM Requests

This appendix presents three instances in 2012 when Navy officials testified that a Navy of more than 500 ships would be required to fully meet combatant commander COCOM requests for Navy forces.

March 22, 2012, Hearing

At a March 22, 2012, hearing on Navy readiness before the Readiness subcommittee of the House Armed Services Committee, the following exchange occurred:

> REPRESENTATIVE J. RANDY FORBES:
>
> We have a lot of requests for our combatant commanders—of the validated requests that come from combatant commanders. How many ships would it take in our navy, based on your estimation, to meet all of the validated requests from our commanders, combatant commanders?
>
> VICE ADMIRAL WILLIAM R. BURKE, DEPUTY CHIEF OF NAVAL OPERATIONS FOR FLEET READINESS AND LOGISTICS:
>
> Let me—give me just a minute on that, sir.
>
> FORBES:
>
> Please. And if you'd like, on any of these questions, if you'd rather take them for the record and get back I'm OK with that, too.
>
> BURKE:
>
> I'm—no, I'm happy to answer the question. I just want to make sure I elaborate a little to make sure we get—get the point right.
>
> FORBES:
>
> Please.
>
> BURKE:
>
> The—the combatant commander requests come in to the—to the services, and then the—there's a—a very high number of requirements from the services, or from the—the combatant commanders which are then prioritized and adjudicated by the joint staff.
>
> Essentially, a way to adjudicate supply—a lesser supply and a greater demand. So—so those—of those requests that come in, some are determined to be more valid than others, if you will. But to get to your exact question, of those requests that come in from the combatant commanders, if we ...
>
> (CROSSTALK)

FORBES:

Admiral, could—could I just—on the nomenclature, just make sure I'm right, too. As they come in, one of the first weed-out processes is we determine whether they're validated or not. In other words, we go through and make sure they're legal, they don't have the other asset somewhere. And—and then we stamp them as validated.

And then like you said, they go through a process where we then look at the resources we have and allocate what we can. And we adjudicate which ones we can give and which ones we can't. So I want the top number. The—the ones that we have validated and said, "Yes, this is legal, it's a proper request."

Of those combatant commander requests, approximately how many ships would it take us to be able to meet those if we had them?

BURKE:

It would take a navy of over 500 ships to meet the combatant commander requests. And, of course, it would take a similar increase in the aircraft and—and other parts of the—of the Navy, as well, to meet the combatant commander requests.[55]

March 29, 2012, Hearing

At a March 29, 2012, hearing on Navy shipbuilding programs before the Seapower and Projection Forces subcommittee of the House Armed Services Committee, the following exchange occurred:

REPRESENTATIVE DUNCAN D. HUNTER:

If you were to build the amphibs [i.e., amphibious ships] where would you prioritize? I mean, where would you take money out of to be able to get the Marine Corps to where they need to be?

VICE ADMIRAL JOHN TERENCE BLAKE, DEPUTY CHIEF OF NAVAL OPERATIONS FOR INTEGRATION OF CAPABILITIES AND RESOURCES:

Here's the issue we deal with: I don't have the luxury of dealing with any single issue in isolation; I have to deal with it across the entire...

HUNTER:

Well, we can. That's why I'm asking.

BLAKE:

Well, we have to deal with it, though, across the entire portfolio.

HUNTER:

Sure.

---

[55] Source: Transcript of hearing.

BLAKE:

And so what we have to do is we have to balance the requirement for amphibs, the requirement for surface combatants, the requirement for the carriers, the submarines—every category of ships that we have. And so when we do that we then have to say, all right, as we balance across that where are we going to be able to assume more risk? And that's how we—that's how we end up where we are.

HUNTER:

So you're saying there is less risk but still risk in the Marine Corps being short on amphibs than there are in the other—the rest of the picture?

BLAKE:

No. I'm saying that we have assumed risk in all areas. The best example I can give you: It was only a short time ago, if we tried to fill all the COCOM needs we said the number was around 400 ships we'd need in the fleet. Today—and we see no abatement in that commitment or the...

HUNTER:

No (inaudible) signal.

BLAKE:

Today we look at it and we see that we would—if we wanted to hit 100 percent of all the COCOM requirements we'd need in excess of 500 ships. So what we end up having to do is we go through the—the global management process and we look at it and we say, here are our highest priorities, these are how we are going to address them, and then we—we have those units available and we push that...

HUNTER:

I understand.

I'm going to yield back in just one second.

So I would take from your statement, then, that you did go through a prioritization process and the amphibs are not at the top of that list. And second, when you say that you assume risk all the way around I would argue that when you do your risk assessment and you prioritize your needs the fact that the COCOMs wanted more ships and needed more ships due to the international environment and where we find ourselves with the world today, going down is probably – it's going the wrong way.

We all know that, but I—I would—I would argue that your prioritization—I would like to see that, if you don't mind, the—the way that you analyzed this and the—and the way that you said, hey, we're going to—we're going to keep them there to make sure that we have this over here. That's all I'm asking for.

BLAKE:

OK. When we put it together we do it across the entire spectrum; we don't—and by that I mean, as we look at the entire requirement we say, this is what we need to do in order to be able to meet the COCOM demand signal.[56]

April 19, 2012, Hearing

At an April 19, 2012, hearing on Navy shipbuilding programs before the Seapower subcommittee of the Senate Armed Services Committee, the following exchange occurred:

SENATOR ROGER WICKER:

Admiral Burke and General Mills, from an operational perspective, the Navy budget cost for decreases in large amphibious ships among other categories, in my opening statement, I mentioned that the requests from combatant commanders for amphibious ships has increased over 80 percent in the last five years—a very dramatic number. What is the reason for that and what will be the impact if these requests are—are not met?

VICE ADMIRAL WILLIAM R. BURKE, DEPUTY CHIEF OF NAVAL OPERATIONS FOR FLEET READINESS AND LOGISTICS:

Senator, thanks for the question. You're right, the COCOM demand signal has gone up significantly to the point where if we were to meet their—all their requirements, it would take a Navy of greater than 500 ships.

So, I certainly am not here to begrudge the COCOM demand signal because they have challenges that they're trying to deal with. But—but we can't meet—meet all their demands. So there is a process in the—in the Pentagon run by the joint staff called the Global Force Management process by which they take in the COCOM requirements and adjudicate that along with the forces we have to come to a reasonable allocation of—of force. And so that's the—that's a process we're dealing with today. We've been using that process for a number of years, and I would expect we will continue to use that process in the future to—to bridge the gap between supply and demand.[57]

---

[56] Source: Transcript of hearing.

[57] Source: Transcript of hearing.

Appendix B. Comparing Past Ship Force Levels to Current or Potential Future Ship Force Levels

In assessing the appropriateness of the current or potential future number of ships in the Navy, observers sometimes compare that number to historical figures for total Navy fleet size. Historical figures for total fleet size, however, can be a problematic yardstick for assessing the appropriateness of the current or potential future number of ships in the Navy, particularly if the historical figures are more than a few years old, because

- the missions to be performed by the Navy, the mix of ships that make up the Navy, and the technologies that are available to Navy ships for performing missions all change over time; and

- the number of ships in the fleet in an earlier year might itself have been inappropriate (i.e., not enough or more than enough) for the meeting the Navy's mission requirements in that year.

Regarding the first bullet point above, the Navy, for example, reached a late-Cold War peak of 568 battle force ships at the end of FY1987,[58] and as of November 8, 2013, included a total of 285 battle force ships. The FY1987 fleet, however, was intended to meet a set of mission requirements that focused on countering Soviet naval forces at sea during a potential multi-theater NATO-Warsaw Pact conflict, while the November 2013 fleet is intended to meet a considerably different set of mission requirements centered on influencing events ashore by countering both land- and sea-based military forces of potential regional threats other than Russia, including improved Chinese military forces and non-state terrorist organizations. In addition, the Navy of FY1987 differed substantially from the November 2013 fleet in areas such as profusion of precision-guided air-delivered weapons, numbers of Tomahawk-capable ships, and the sophistication of C4ISR systems and networking capabilities.[59]

In coming years, Navy missions may shift again, and the capabilities of Navy ships will likely have changed further by that time due to developments such as more comprehensive implementation of networking technology, increased use of ship-based unmanned vehicles, and the potential fielding of new types of weapons such as lasers or electromagnetic rail guns.

The 568-ship fleet of FY1987 may or may not have been capable of performing its stated missions; the 285-ship fleet of November 2013 may or may not be capable of performing its stated missions; and a fleet years from now with a certain number of ships may or may not be capable of performing its stated missions. Given changes over time in mission requirements, ship

---

[58] Some publications have stated that the Navy reached a peak of 594 ships at the end of FY1987. This figure, however, is the total number of active ships in the fleet, which is not the same as the total number of battle force ships. The battle force ships figure is the number used in government discussions of the size of the Navy. In recent years, the total number of active ships has been larger than the total number of battle force ships. For example, the Naval History and Heritage Command (formerly the Naval Historical Center) states that as of November 16, 2001, the Navy included a total of 337 active ships, while the Navy states that as of November 19, 2001, the Navy included a total of 317 battle force ships. Comparing the total number of active ships in one year to the total number of battle force ships in another year is thus an apples-to-oranges comparison that in this case overstates the decline since FY1987 in the number of ships in the Navy. As a general rule to avoid potential statistical distortions, comparisons of the number of ships in the Navy over time should use, whenever possible, a single counting method.

[59] C4ISR stands for command and control, communications, computers, intelligence, surveillance, and reconnaissance.

mixes, and technologies, however, these three issues are to a substantial degree independent of one another.

For similar reasons, trends over time in the total number of ships in the Navy are not necessarily a reliable indicator of the direction of change in the fleet's ability to perform its stated missions. An increasing number of ships in the fleet might not necessarily mean that the fleet's ability to perform its stated missions is increasing, because the fleet's mission requirements might be increasing more rapidly than ship numbers and average ship capability. Similarly, a decreasing number of ships in the fleet might not necessarily mean that the fleet's ability to perform stated missions is decreasing, because the fleet's mission requirements might be declining more rapidly than numbers of ships, or because average ship capability and the percentage of time that ships are in deployed locations might be increasing quickly enough to more than offset reductions in total ship numbers.

Regarding the second of the two bullet points above, it can be noted that comparisons of the size of the fleet today with the size of the fleet in earlier years rarely appear to consider whether the fleet was appropriately sized in those earlier years (and therefore potentially suitable as a yardstick of comparison), even though it is quite possible that the fleet in those earlier years might not have been appropriately sized, and even though there might have been differences of opinion among observers at that time regarding that question. Just as it might not be prudent for observers years from now to tacitly assume that the 285-ship of November 2013 was appropriately sized for meeting the mission requirements of 2013, even though there currently are differences of opinion among observers on that question (as reflected, for example, in **Table 7**) simply because a figure of 285 ships appears in the historical records for 2013, so, too, might it not be prudent for observers today to tacitly assume that the number of ships of the Navy in an earlier year was appropriate for meeting the Navy's mission requirements that year, even though there might have been differences of opinion among observers at that time regarding that question, simply because the size of the Navy in that year appears in a table like **Table D-1**.

Previous Navy force structure plans, such as those shown in **Table 1**, might provide some insight into the potential adequacy of a proposed new force-structure plan, but changes over time in mission requirements, technologies available to ships for performing missions, and other force-planning factors, as well as the possibility that earlier force-structure plans might not have been appropriate for meeting the mission demands of their times, suggest that some caution should be applied in using past force structure plans for this purpose, particularly if those past force structure plans are more than a few years old. The Reagan-era plan for a 600-ship Navy, for example, was designed for a Cold War set of missions focusing on countering Soviet naval forces at sea, which is not an appropriate basis for planning the Navy today, and there was considerable debate during those years as to the appropriateness of the 600-ship goal.[60]

---

[60] Navy force structure plans that predate those shown in **Table 1** include the Reagan-era 600-ship plan of the 1980s, the Base Force fleet of more than 400 ships planned during the final two years of the George H. W. Bush Administration, the 346-ship fleet from the Clinton Administration's 1993 Bottom-Up Review (or BUR, sometimes also called Base Force II), and the 310-ship fleet of the Clinton Administration's 1997 QDR. The table below summarizes some key features of these plans.

Features of Recent Navy Force Structure Plans

Plan	600-ship	Base Force	1993 BUR	1997 QDR
Total ships	~600	~450/416[a]	346	~305/310[b]
Attack submarines	100	80/~55[c]	45-55	50/55[d]

(continued...)

Appendix C. Independent Panel Assessment of 2010 QDR

The law that requires DOD to perform QDRs once every four years (10 U.S.C. 118) states that the results of each QDR shall be assessed by an independent panel. The report of the independent panel that assessed the 2010 QDR was released on July 29, 2010. The independent panel's report recommended a Navy of 346 ships, including 11 aircraft carriers and 55 attack submarines.[61] The report stated the following, among other things:

- "The QDR should reflect current commitments, but it must also plan effectively for potential threats that could arise over the next 20 years.... we believe the 2010 QDR did not accord sufficient priority to the need to counter anti-access challenges, strengthen homeland defense (including our defense against cyber threats), and conduct post-conflict stabilization missions." (Page 54)

- "In this remarkable period of change, global security will still depend upon an American presence capable of unimpeded access to all international areas of the Pacific region. In an environment of 'anti-access strategies,' and assertions to create unique 'economic and security zones of influence,' America's rightful and historic presence will be critical. To preserve our interests, the United States will need to retain the ability to transit freely the areas of the Western Pacific for security and economic reasons. Our allies also depend on us to be fully present in the Asia-Pacific as a promoter of stability and to ensure the free flow of commerce. A robust U.S. force structure, largely rooted in maritime strategy but including other necessary capabilities, will be essential." (Page 51)

- "The United States will need agile forces capable of operating against the full range of potential contingencies. However, the need to deal with irregular and hybrid threats will tend to drive the size and shape of ground forces for years to

(...continued)				
Aircraft carriers	15[e]	12	11+1[f]	11+1[f]
Surface combatants	242/228[g]	~150	~124	116
Amphibious ships	~75[h]	51[i]	41[i]	36[i]

Source: Prepared by CRS based on DOD and U.S. Navy data.
a. Commonly referred to as 450-ship plan, but called for decreasing to 416 ships by end of FY1999.
b. Original total of about 305 ships was increased to about 310 due to increase in number of attack submarines to 55 from 50.
c. Plan originally included 80 attack submarines, but this was later reduced to about 55.
d. Plan originally included 50 attack submarines but this was later increased to 55.
e. Plus one additional aircraft carrier in the service life extension program (SLEP).
f. Eleven active carriers plus one operational reserve carrier.
g. Plan originally included 242 surface combatants but this was later reduced to 228.
h. Number needed to lift assault echelons of one Marine Expeditionary Force (MEF) plus one Marine Expeditionary Brigade (MEB).
i. Number needed to lift assault echelons of 2.5 MEBs. Changing numbers needed to meet this goal reflect in part changes in the design and capabilities of amphibious ships.

[61] Stephen J. Hadley and William J. Perry, co-chairmen, et al, *The QDR in Perspective: Meeting America's National Security Needs In the 21st Century, The Final Report of the Quadrennial Defense Review Independent Panel*, Washington, 2010, Figure 3-2 on page 58.

come, whereas the need to continue to be fully present in Asia and the Pacific and other areas of interest will do the same for naval and air forces." (Page 55)

- "The force structure in the Asia-Pacific needs to be increased. In order to preserve U.S. interests, the United States will need to retain the ability to transit freely the areas of the Western Pacific for security and economic reasons. The United States must be fully present in the Asia-Pacific region to protect American lives and territory, ensure the free flow of commerce, maintain stability, and defend our allies in the region. A robust U.S. force structure, one that is largely rooted in maritime strategy and includes other necessary capabilities, will be essential." (Page 66)

- "Force structure must be strengthened in a number of areas to address the need to counter anti-access challenges, strengthen homeland defense (including defense against cyber threats), and conduct post-conflict stabilization missions: First, as a Pacific power, the U.S. presence in Asia has underwritten the regional stability that has enabled India and China to emerge as rising economic powers. The United States should plan on continuing that role for the indefinite future. The Panel remains concerned that the QDR force structure may not be sufficient to assure others that the United States can meet its treaty commitments in the face of China's increased military capabilities. Therefore, we recommend an increased priority on defeating anti-access and area-denial threats. This will involve acquiring new capabilities, and, as Secretary Gates has urged, developing innovative concepts for their use. Specifically, we believe the United States must fully fund the modernization of its surface fleet. We also believe the United States must be able to deny an adversary sanctuary by providing persistent surveillance, tracking, and rapid engagement with high-volume precision strike. That is why the Panel supports an increase in investment in long-range strike systems and their associated sensors. In addition, U.S. forces must develop and demonstrate the ability to operate in an information-denied environment." (Pages 59-60)

- "To compete effectively, the U.S. military must continue to develop new conceptual approaches to dealing with operational challenges, like the Capstone Concept for Joint Operations (CCJO). The Navy and Air Force's effort to develop an Air-Sea Battle concept is one example of an approach to deal with the growing anti-access challenge. It will be necessary to invest in modernized capabilities to make this happen. The Chief of Naval Operations and Chief of Staff of the Air Force deserve support in this effort, and the Panel recommends the other military services be brought into the concept when appropriate." (Page 51; a similar passage appears on page 67)

In recommending a Navy of 346 ships, the independent panel's report cited the 1993 Bottom-Up Review (BUR) of U.S. defense plans and policies. **Table C-1** compares the Navy's 306-ship goal of March 2012 to the 346-ship Navy recommended in the 1993 BUR (as detailed partly in subsequent Navy testimony and publications) and the ship force levels recommended in the independent panel report.

Table C-1. Comparison of Navy's 306-ship goal, Navy Plan from 1993 BUR, and Navy Plan from 2010 QDR Review Panel

Ship Type	Navy's 306-ship goal of March 2012	Bottom-Up Review (BUR) (1993)	2010 QDR Independent Review Panel (July 2010)
SSBNs	12-14	18	14
		(SSBN force was later reduced to 14 as a result of the 1994 Nuclear Posture Review)	
SSGNs	0-4	0	4
		(SSGN program did not yet exist)	
SSNs	~48	45 to 55	55
		(55 in FY99, with a long-term goal of about 45)	
Aircraft carriers	11 active	11 active + 1 operational/reserve	11 active
Surface combatants	~145	124	n/a
		(114 active + 10 frigates in Naval Reserve Force; a total of 110-116 active ships was also cited)	
Cruisers and destroyers	*~90*	*n/a*	*n/a*
Frigates	*0*	*n/a*	*n/a*
	(to be replaced by LCSs)		
LCSs	*~55*	*0*	*n/a*
		(LCS program did not exist)	
Amphibious ships	~32	41	n/a
	(30 operational ships needed to lift 2.0 MEBs)	(Enough to lift 2.5 MEBs)	
Dedicated mine warfare ships	0	26	n/a
	(to be replaced by LCSs)	(LCS program did not exist)	
CLF ships	~29	43	n/a
Support ships	~33	22	n/a
TOTAL ships	**~306**	**346**	**346**
		(numbers above add to 331-341)[a]	

Source: Table prepared by CRS. ***Sources for 1993 Bottom-Up Review:*** Department of Defense, *Report on the Bottom-Up Review*, October 1993, Figure 7 on page 28; Department of the Navy, *Highlights of the FY 1995 Department of the Navy Budget*, February 1994, p. 1; Department of the Navy, *Force 2001, A Program Guide to the U.S. Navy*, 1994 edition, p. 15; Statement of VADM T. Joseph Lopez, U.S. Navy, Deputy Chief of Naval Operations (Resources, Warfare Requirements & Assessments), Testimony to the Military Forces and Personnel Subcommittee of the House Armed Services Committee, March 22, 1994, pp. 2-5. ***Source for independent panel report:*** Stephen J. Hadley and William J. Perry, co-chairmen, et al., *The QDR in Perspective: Meeting*

America's National Security Needs In the 21st Century, The Final Report of the Quadrennial Defense Review Independent Panel, Washington, 2010, Figure 3-2 on pages 58-59.

Notes: n/a is not addressed in the report. **SSBN** is nuclear-powered ballistic missile submarine; **SSGN** is nuclear-powered cruise missile and special operations forces submarine; **SSN** is nuclear-powered attack submarine; **LCS** is Littoral Combat Ship; **MPF(F)** is Maritime Prepositioning Force (Future) ship; **CLF** is combat logistics force (i.e., resupply) ship; **MEB** is Marine Expeditionary Brigade.

a. The Navy testified in 1994 that the planned number was adjusted from 346 to 330 to reflect reductions in numbers of tenders and early retirements of some older amphibious ships.

In a letter dated August 11, 2010, Secretary of Defense Robert Gates provided his comments on the independent panel's report. The letter stated in part:

> I completely agree with the Panel that a strong navy is essential; however, I disagree with the Panel's recommendation that DoD should establish the 1993 Bottom Up Review's (BUR's) fleet of 346 ships as the objective target. That number was a simple projection of the then-planned size of [the] Navy in FY 1999, not a reflection of 21st century, steady-state requirements. The fleet described in the 2010 QDR report, with its overall target of 313 to 321 ships, has roughly the same number of aircraft carriers, nuclear-powered attack submarines, surface combatants, mine warfare vessels, and amphibious ships as the larger BUR fleet. The main difference between the two fleets is in the numbers of combat logistics, mobile logistics, and support ships. Although it is true that the 2010 fleet includes fewer of these ships, they are all now more efficiently manned and operated by the Military Sealift Command and meet all of DoD's requirements....
>
> I agree with the Panel's general conclusion that DoD ought to enhance its overall posture and capabilities in the Asia-Pacific region. As I outlined in my speech at the Naval War College in April 2009, "to carry out the missions we may face in the future... we will need numbers, speed, and the ability to operate in shallow waters." So as the Air-Sea battle concept development reaches maturation, and as DoD's review of global defense posture continues, I will be looking for ways to meet plausible security threats while emphasizing sustained forward presence – particularly in the Pacific.[62]

---

[62] Letter dated August 11, 2010, from Secretary of Defense Robert Gates to the chairmen of the House and Senate Armed Services and Appropriations Committees, pp. 3 and 4. The ellipsis in the second paragraph appears in the letter.

Appendix D. Size of the Navy and Navy Shipbuilding Rate

Size of the Navy

Table D-1 shows the size of the Navy in terms of total number of ships since FY1948; the numbers shown in the table reflect changes over time in the rules specifying which ships count toward the total. Differing counting rules result in differing totals, and for certain years, figures reflecting more than one set of counting rules are available. Figures in the table for FY1978 and subsequent years reflect the battle force ships counting method, which is the set of counting rules established in the early 1980s for public policy discussions of the size of the Navy.

As shown in the table, the total number of battle force ships in the Navy reached a late-Cold War peak of 568 at the end of FY1987 and began declining thereafter.[63] The Navy fell below 300 battle force ships in August 2003 and included 285 battle force ships as of November 8, 2013.

As discussed in **Appendix B**, historical figures for total fleet size might not be a reliable yardstick for assessing the appropriateness of proposals for the future size and structure of the Navy, particularly if the historical figures are more than a few years old, because the missions to be performed by the Navy, the mix of ships that make up the Navy, and the technologies that are available to Navy ships for performing missions all change over time, and because the number of ships in the fleet in an earlier year might itself have been inappropriate (i.e., not enough or more than enough) for the meeting the Navy's mission requirements in that year.

For similar reasons, trends over time in the total number of ships in the Navy are not necessarily a reliable indicator of the direction of change in the fleet's ability to perform its stated missions. An increasing number of ships in the fleet might not necessarily mean that the fleet's ability to perform its stated missions is increasing, because the fleet's mission requirements might be increasing more rapidly than ship numbers and average ship capability. Similarly, a decreasing number of ships in the fleet might not necessarily mean that the fleet's ability to perform stated missions is decreasing, because the fleet's mission requirements might be declining more rapidly than numbers of ships, or because average ship capability and the percentage of time that ships are in deployed locations might be increasing quickly enough to more than offset reductions in total ship numbers.

---

[63] Some publications have stated that the Navy reached a peak of 594 ships at the end of FY1987. This figure, however, is the total number of active ships in the fleet, which is not the same as the total number of battle force ships. The battle force ships figure is the number used in government discussions of the size of the Navy. In recent years, the total number of active ships has been larger than the total number of battle force ships. For example, the Naval History and Heritage Command (formerly the Naval Historical Center) states that as of November 16, 2001, the Navy included a total of 337 active ships, while the Navy states that as of November 19, 2001, the Navy included a total of 317 battle force ships. Comparing the total number of active ships in one year to the total number of battle force ships in another year is thus an apples-to-oranges comparison that in this case overstates the decline since FY1987 in the number of ships in the Navy. As a general rule to avoid potential statistical distortions, comparisons of the number of ships in the Navy over time should use, whenever possible, a single counting method.

Table D-1. Total Number of Ships in the Navy Since FY1948

FY[a]	Number	FY[a]	Number	FY[a]	Number
1948	737	1970	769	1992	466
1949	690	1971	702	1993	435
1950	634	1972	654	1994	391
1951	980	1973	584	1995	373
1952	1,097	1974	512	1996	356
1953	1,122	1975	496	1997	354
1954	1,113	1976	476	1998	333
1955	1,030	1977	464	1999	317
1956	973	1978	468	2000	318
1957	967	1979	471	2001	316
1958	890	1980	477	2002	313
1959	860	1981	490	2003	297
1960	812	1982	513	2004	291
1961	897	1983	514	2005	282
1962	959	1984	524	2006	281
1963	916	1985	541	2007	279
1964	917	1986	556	2008	282
1965	936	1987	568	2009	285
1966	947	1988	565	2010	288
1967	973	1989	566	2011	284
1968	976	1990	547	2012	287
1969	926	1991	526	2013	

Source: Compiled by CRS using U.S. Navy data. Numbers shown reflect changes over time in the rules specifying which ships count toward the total. Figures for FY1978 and subsequent years reflect the battle force ships counting method, which is the set of counting rules established in the early 1980s for public policy discussions of the size of the Navy.

a. Data for earlier years in the table may be for the end of the calendar year (or for some other point during the year), rather than for the end of the fiscal year.

Shipbuilding Rate

Table D-2 shows past (FY1982-FY2013) and requested (FY2014-FY2018) rates of Navy ship procurement.

Table D-2. Battle Force Ships Procured or Requested, FY1982-FY2018

(Procured FY1982-FY2013; requested FY2014-FY2018)

82	83	84	85	86	87	88	89	90	91	92	93	94	95	96	97	98	99	00
17	14	16	19	20	17	15	19	15	11	11	7	4	4	5	4	5	5	6

01	02	03	04	05	06	07	08	09	10	11	12	13	14	15	16	17	18
6	6	5	7	8	4a	5a	3a	8	7	10	11b	11c	8	8	7	9	9

Source: CRS compilation based on Navy budget data and examination of defense authorization and appropriation committee and conference reports for each fiscal year. The table excludes non-battle force ships that do not count toward the 306-ship goal, such as certain sealift and prepositioning ships operated by the Military Sealift Command and oceanographic ships operated by agencies such as the National Oceanic and Atmospheric Administration (NOAA).

a. The totals shown for FY2006, FY2007, and FY2008, reflect the cancellation two LCSs funded in FY2006, another two LCSs funded in FY2007, and an LCS funded in FY2008.

b. The total shown for FY2012 includes two JHSVs—one that was included in the Navy's FY2012 budget submission, and one that was included in the Army's FY2012 budget submission. Until FY2012, JHSVs were being procured by both the Navy and the Army. The Army was to procure its fifth and final JHSV in FY2012, and this ship was included in the Army's FY2012 budget submission. In May 2011, the Navy and Army signed a Memorandum of Agreement (MOA) transferring the Army's JHSVs to the Navy. In the FY2012 DOD Appropriations Act (Division A of H.R. 2055/P.L. 112-74 of December 23, 2011), the JHSV that was in the Army's FY2012 budget submission was funded through the Shipbuilding and Conversion, Navy (SCN) appropriation account, along with the JHSV that the Navy had included in its FY0212 budget submission. The four JHSVs that were procured through the Army's budget prior to FY2012, however, are *not* included in the annual totals shown in this table.

c. Figure shown does not reflect potential quantity reduction resulting from March 1, 2013, sequester on FY2013 funding.

Author Contact Information

Ronald O'Rourke
Specialist in Naval Affairs
rorourke@crs.loc.gov, 7-7610